Learnings
Lessons We Are Learning About Living Together

Edited
By
Dave Andrews and Helen Beazley

WIPF & STOCK · Eugene, Oregon

Wipf and Stock Publishers
199 W 8th Ave, Suite 3
Eugene, OR 97401

Learnings
Lessons We Are Learning About Living Together
By Andrews, Dave and Beazley, Helen
Copyright©2010 by Andrews, Dave
ISBN 13: 978-1-61097-853-8
Publication date 2/1/2012
Previously published by Last First Networks, 2010

Introduction to Dave Andrews for the 2012 Dave Andrews Legacy Series

I KEPT seeing this guy on the shuttle bus - long hair, graying beard, a gentle 60's-70's feel to him. He seemed thoughtful, intense, friendly, and quiet, like he had a lot on his mind, as did I. Even though I saw him nearly every time I boarded the shuttle bus, we didn't speak beyond him smiling and saying, "G'day" and me nodding and saying, "Hey" as we boarded or disembarked.

It was my first time at Greenbelt, a huge festival about faith, art, and justice held every August in the UK. I had always heard great things about the event and so was thrilled when I was invited to speak. I was just as thrilled to get a chance to hear in person some musicians and speakers I had only heard about from a distance, so I went through the program and marked people I wanted to be sure not to miss.

It was near the end of the conference when a friend told me to be sure to catch an Australian fellow named Dave Andrews. "I've never heard of him," I said. "Oh, he's a force of nature," my friend said. "Kind of like Jim Wallis, Tony Campolo, and Mother Teresa rolled up into one." How could I not put a combination like that in one of the last free slots on my schedule?

I arrived at the venue a few minutes late and there he was, the bearded guy from the bus. Thoughtful, intense, and friendly, yes - but *quiet* he was not. He was nearly exploding with passion - passion and compassion, in a voice that ranged from fortissimo to fortississimo to furioso. How could a guy churning with so much hope, love, anger, energy, faith, fury, and curiosity have been so quiet and unassuming on the bus?

He was a force of nature indeed, evoking from his audience laughter, shouts, amens, reverent silence, and even tears before he was done. He spoke of justice, of poverty, of oppression, of solidarity across religious differences, of service, of hope, of celebration, of the way of Jesus.

As I listened, I wanted to kick myself. *This is the most inspiring talk I've heard at this whole festival. Why did I miss all those opportunities to get to know this fellow on the bus? Now the festival is almost over and I've missed my chance!*

Later than evening, I boarded the shuttle bus for the last ride back to my hotel, and there sat Dave and his wife, Ange. I didn't miss my chance this time. I introduced myself and they reciprocated warmly.

I was a largely unknown American author at the time and hardly known at Greenbelt, much less in Australia, so I'm quite certain Dave and Ange had never heard of me. But they couldn't have been kinder, and as we disembarked, he pulled two books from his backpack and told me they were a gift.

The next day when I flew home from Heathrow, I devoured them both on the plane. First, I opened *Not Religion, But Love* and read it through from cover to cover. Then I opened *Christi-anarchy* and couldn't put it down either. When my plane landed, I felt I had been on a spiritual retreat . . . or maybe better said, in a kind of spiritual boot camp!

Things I was thinking but had been afraid to say out loud Dave was saying boldly and confidently. Ideas I was very tentatively considering he had already been living with for years. Complaints and concerns I only shared in highly guarded situations he was publishing from the housetops. Hopes and ideals I didn't dare to express he celebrated without embarrassment.

I think I gave him a copy of one or two of my books as well, and I guess he was favorably impressed enough that we stayed in touch and a friendship developed. I discovered that we were both songwriters as well as writers, that we both had a deep interest in interfaith friendships, that we both had some critics and we both had known the pain of labeling and rejection.

Since then, whatever he has written, I've been sure to read . . . knowing that he speaks to my soul in a way that nobody else does.

We've managed to get together several times since our initial meeting in England, in spite of the fact that we live on opposite sides of the planet. We've spoken together at a few conferences on both hemispheres, and I had the privilege of visiting him in Brisbane. I've seen the beautiful things he has been doing in a particularly interesting and challenging neighborhood there, walking the streets with him, meeting his friends, sensing his love for that place and those people. He's been in my home in the US as well, and we've been conspiring for some other chances to be and work together in the future.

In my speaking across North America, I frequently refer to Dave's work, but until now, his books have been hard to come by. That's why I'm thrilled to introduce this volume to everyone I can in North America.

Yes, you'll find he's one part Tony Campolo, one part Jim Wallis, and one part Mother Teresa, a force of nature, as I was told.

You'll also find he is a serious student of the Bible and a serious theological sage — the kind of reflective activist or thinker-practitioner that we need more of.

In a book like *Christi-anarchy*, he can boldly and provocatively unsettle you and challenge you. Then in a book like *Plan Be*, he can gently and pastorally encourage and inspire you. Like the central inspiration of his life, he is the kind of person to confidently turn over tables in the Temple one minute and then humbly defend a shamed and abused woman from her accusers the next.

You'll see in Dave's writings that he is highly knowledgeable about poverty, ecology, psychology, sociology, politics, and economics . . . not only from an academic standpoint, but also from a grassroots, experiential level. His writing on these subjects grows from what he has done on the ground . . . for example, nurturing a community network that is training young adults to live and serve among the poor, supervising homes for adults who are learning to live with physical and psychiatric disabilities, encouraging small businesses to hire people who others would consider unemployable and developing a non-profit solar energy co-op for local people.

Dave's writings and friendship have meant so much to me. I consider him a friend and mentor. Now I am so happy that people across North America can discover him too.

You'll feel as I did — so grateful that you didn't miss the chance to learn from this one-of-a-kind, un-categorizable, un-containable, wild wonder from Down Under named Dave Andrews.

Brian D. McLaren
author/speaker/activist (brianmclaren.net)

Contents

Introduction

Foreword   7
Lin Hatfield Dodds

Acknowledgements   13

The Network

What is the Waiters Union?   15
Dave Andrews and Helen Beazley

'The Thing I Have Held Most Dear Through The Years'   21
Angie Andrews

'A Ready Made Community Network'   33
Steve Collins-Haynes

'I Cannot See Myself Living Anywhere Else'   35
Sannie Pritchard

'A Local's Evaluation Of The Waiters Union'   43
Stephanie Becker

The Training

What training do people in the Waiters Union provide?   51
Dave Andrews and Helen Beazley

'An Open Letter About The Input'   61
Ashley Withers

'Personal Reflections On The Experience'   63
John Dacey

'Why We Send Our Staff For Training'   67
Diane and Ross Coleman

The Learnings

What learnings do people derive from the Waiters Union?   69
Dave Andrews and Helen Beazley

Contents

'Living And Learning In The Waiters Union'   79
Helen Beazley

'Learning Theology Through Conversation'   81
Leanne Baker

'Learning About Reality Through Immersion'   85
Pete Hawkins

'Learning To Be Real Through Experimentation'   91
Peter Noble

'A Visitor's View Of The Waiters Union'   95
Nicholas Fiedler

'Falling Down The Waiters Union Rabbit Hole'   101
Emily James

'Air, Water, Earth, Fire And The Waiters Union'   105
Marty Richards

'Songs, Guitars, Rockstars And The Waiters Union'   109
Peter Branjerdporn

'Hippies, Ideals, Realities And The Waiters Union'   113
Christel Palmer

'Love, Adventure, Nonviolence And The Waiters Union'   117
Jason MacLeod

'Ways We Have Learnt To Walk With Indigenous Australians'   125
Neil Hockey

'Ways We Have Learnt To Work With Refugees in Australia'   133
Angie Andrews

'A National Park For Aussie Christians'   141
Lin Hatfield Dodds

'A Safe Place For Radical Conversations'   147
Charles Ringma

Contents

'A Reference Point For Radical Christians'   151
Greg Gow

'The Waiters Union And Christian Anarchy'   155
Jim Dowling and Anne Rampa

'The Waiters Union And The Traditional Church'   161
Craig Mischiewski

'The Waiters Union And The Emerging Church'   165
Steve Drinkall

'The Waiters Union And Local Mission'   171
Kenn Baker

'The Waiters Union And International Mission'   177
Mark Delaney

'The Waiters Union And Intentional Community'   183
Noritta Morseu-Diop

'The Waiters Union And Community Development'   189
Peter Westoby

'The Waiters, Local Power And Community Sustainability'   197
Rob Farago and Russ Holmes

'The Waiters, Vibrant Spirituality And Social Justice'   203
Armen Gakavian

'The Experience Of Pain And The Possibility Of Change'   211
Maddie Anlezark

'Being The Change We Want To See In The World'   217
Cara Munroe

End Notes

Waiters Union Liturgy   225
Waiters Union Activities   227
The Community Initiatives Resource Association   231
The Community Praxis Co-op   233

Foreword

In the early 1990s my partner Steve and I spent a summer in Brisbane's West End, participating in the life of the local community as part of the Waiters Union community immersion experience. How did two university educated middleclass young public servants from Canberra end up flicking off cockroaches climbing up their legs while showering in a dodgy boarding house in inner city Brisbane? What sort of idiots choose to spend their annual leave serving in a community soup kitchen and visiting men in a maximum security prison rather than sunbathing on a beach a fair bit further north?

We had both been shaped in families of origin and church communities that were focused out rather than in, that linked love and grace to solidarity and service. But in our early twenties we were struggling with what it meant to be people of faith living a privileged life in the developed West and wondering what taking risks and living hope-fully could mean in our context. What was our call to stand and love with Christ at the edges?

A friend lent us *Can You Hear The Heartbeat?* and we found in its pages a group that was seriously and practically engaged with the vocation of love at the edges – the Waiters Union. What we glimpsed in that book was a community of friends trying to live out one of the most elegant and gut grabbing expressions of the Christian dream that we had ever encountered – radical, communitarian, grounded in compassion. We wanted to explore moving beyond supporting the activism of others to becoming activists ourselves, and we wanted to explore that in a community that was living out a radical response to love and grace.

So we got organised and got on a plane to Brisbane. The Waiters Union course itself was a really great mix of a range of inputs from people with expertise and experience in working with vulnerable and disadvantaged communities and us getting involved ourselves. We lived in a community house and mornings were mostly spent in small group discussion and learning while afternoons and evenings were spent in the community, serving in the local soup kitchen, delivering meals on wheels, playing sport in the park with refugee families, and visiting the prison.

Sometimes it felt like being thrown in at the deep end with no lifevest. Like when we had to accommodate ourselves for a week on about $70. For two of us. Steve and I ended up in a dodgy boarding house listening to domestic violence being enacted in the room next to ours most nights. That's the place we discovered the delights of sharing a shower with a few cockroaches. I remember thinking "What am I learning here?" It turns out that I learnt, experientially, possibly the most important lesson of my life: that the kind of life I live, full of love and open doors to opportunity, is not enjoyed by an appallingly high proportion of our community.

While the truth of what life is like for people who are left out and missing out was a keystone learning, we learnt heaps of other stuff that summer. Spending time with the Waiters Union gave me a framework and a basic toolkit to build from. Here's a grab bag of lessons I learnt:

> *Poverty and social isolation go hand in hand. Low self esteem, depression, and poor health can follow pretty rapidly.*
>
> *It is possible to live with dignity and hope in poverty but this possibility is more likely to be realised if you have a community to support and encourage you.*
>
> *Relationship is everything. Apologies matter. The capacity*

to forgive seems linked to the experience of suffering.

Transition moments – a birth, a death, a move, a new job, a new school, an illness – provide opportunities to journey with others, building community.

Local community is critical to social transformation.

Service and solidarity form part of a two way street. You always, but always, learn from, and are transformed by, any relational encounter.

Policy developed in airconditioned offices far from the lived reality of people struggling in poverty, with disabilities, with episodic mental illness or other barriers to participation in community will often be at best ineffective and at worst actively unhelpful.

The institutions that sustain us – church, government have too often been institutions of oppression for the vulnerable in Australia – Aboriginal people, children in care, people with disabilities, gay people. Usually when "doing to" rather than "journeying with."

What seems too confronting one day will often be normalised the next. People are endlessly adaptive. So holding onto some bottom lines about what is acceptable (open friendship) and what is not (endemic poverty) in a wealthy nation like ours is important, as is understanding that we can all do something where we are with what we have to make a difference.

> *Radical activism must be focused on unjust systems. There have always been resistors of oppression within the system. The resistor narrative is the heart of the story of hope.*
>
> *The meta-narrative of the Christian story is a solid and tested one for working toward justice, hope, and the transformation of all of creation. When you unpack scripture you find a workbook for just living.*

We came home confirmed in our belief that if faith matters at all, it has to matter beyond the congregational or small group experience.

It must matter in all of life. That means reflecting, engaging, and struggling to work out how to apply faith compassionately and respectfully in all of the relationships and activities that make up your week and month and year. Small call!

We came home with a framework for radical discipleship in the developed West, and a new resolve to work where we were toward transforming unjust systems and structures, while actively participating in community.

My beloved dad died last year, far too young at 68. It was cancer, so we had time to talk. One of the most important things he said to me was that he had no regrets, about who he was or how he had spent himself over the course of his very rich life. How many of us could honestly say that?

I want to live and love with no regrets. I want to do my part to leave the world a better place. I want to be an active part of a people's movement for social, political, economic and environmental transformation. I want to see the reconciliation of all of creation.

This book celebrates the learnings of people who journeyed a week, a month, a decade, or more with that small network in West End. It's a celebration of many ordinary everyday people living in and working with communities where not everyone has enough to eat, or a safe place to live, or access to a good education or adequate health care. It's a celebration of an authentic struggle to live grace and hope and love into the world. It's a celebration of a successful people's movement and a life changing community immersion experience.

I hope it is also an encouragement and a resource to help you move from where you are now to where you want to be.

Take a risk, have a go, be the change we so desperately need to see in our world.

You will never regret it.

Lin Hatfield Dodds
Canberra 2010
National Director Uniting Care Australia
Past President Australian Council of Social Service

Acknowledgements

Most books begin with acknowledgements.

We'd like to begin with an acknowledgement of all those who have written reflections for this book which celebrate some of the lessons they have learnt from our community.

But every community has a dark side as well as a light side. And we'd also like to begin this book with an acknowledgement of all those people who would have had difficulty in writing anything celebrating their association with the Waiters Union: people who came to the Waiters with high hopes, but left with deep disappointments; people who didn't experience the Waiters as hospitable or helpful or supportive; people who experienced the Waiters as exclusive, not inclusive, but cliquey – experienced the Waiters as elitist, self-righteous and judgmental of others.

We know that community amplifies our experiences. It makes good experiences better and bad experiences worse. So any pain people may have experienced in the context of the network would have certainly been intense. And we want to acknowledge that.

Having said that, we'd still like to share these bright diamonds mined from the dark coal.

Stories of our successes, wrested from our failures, are the more valuable for being rare.

These reflections highlight the little bit of progress we have made in the midst of our struggle to live with each other and work with one another. These learnings sustain our hope for learning more about how we can move towards a more authentic life together.

Acknowledgements

The very process of publishing a book about our learnings has been a learning process. It has entailed a difficult and complicated conversation about what the book should be about, how we should go about writing it and whom we should invite to write it.

This book is not a history of the Waiters: it does not provide a detailed account of the ups and downs of our journey. The funding from A Vision For Mission given to the Training Team to publish this book was specifically dedicated to reporting on the learnings people have gained from experiencing our training or connecting with the network. Some of the contributors may have only been with the Waiters for a short while and their perspective might be considered by some as partial, incomplete and/or overly romantic.

As part of the Training Team, we invited particular visitors, locals, colleagues and friends, who had expressed their appreciation for the role that the network had played in their lives, to write about their experience – hoping we would get 20 different pieces written by 20 different people about their experiences of the Waiters over the last 20 years. We also put out a general invitation through the Waiters Union Newsletter for contributions.

The bits and pieces people have written for this book represent a beautiful multi-coloured, multi-layered mosaic of lessons they have learnt about living life together through their association with the Waiters Union and their participation in our training.

Dave Andrews and Helen Beazley (editors) West End 2010

The Network
What is the Waiters Union?

Anyone who knows the Waiters Union knows this is a topic of endless discussions and debates. If you asked lots of different people associated with the Waiters Union this question, chances are you'd get lots of different answers. However, there's a good possibility that many of those answers would be variations of the statement that you can find on the home page of www.waitersunion.org which says: "the Waiters Union is a network of residents in West End who are committed to developing a sense of community in the locality with our neighbours, including those who are marginalised, in the radical tradition of Jesus of Nazareth."[1] And most people associated with the Waiters Union would agree with that. More or less.

•

No one is quite sure when the Waiters Union began, but it seems to have emerged sometime after 1985, when Dave and Ange Andrews returned from India to Australia and expressed interest in doing the same kind of faith-based community work in West End as they had done in New Delhi. They were joined by two other couples, Chris and Ruth Todd, and Nigel and Sue Lewin, who had met Dave and Ange in India and moved into the area and helped start the network.

The network was called the West End Waiters Union because we wanted to be waiters in West End. We didn't want to set agendas for people. We wanted to be available, like waiters, to take people's orders and to do what we could do to help them. We particularly wanted to help to develop a sense of hospitality in the locality, so that all people, especially people who are usually displaced in areas like ours, could really begin to feel at home in the community.

---

[1] http://www.waitersunion.org

In the early days people in the network talked a lot about our aspirations. We dreamt of a world in which all the resources of the earth would be shared equally between all the people of the earth so that even the most disadvantaged among us would be able to meet basic needs with dignity and joy. We dreamt of a great society of small communities cooperating interdependently to practise personal, social, economic and political compassion, love, justice and peace. We dreamt of people developing networks of friendships in which the pain we carry deep down could be shared openly in an atmosphere of mutual support and respect. We dreamt of people understanding the difficulties we have in common, discussing our problems, discussing the solutions, and working together for personal growth and social change in the light of the love of Christ. And we yearned to make this dream a reality in our own locality.[2]

As there is no membership, no one is quite sure how many people there are in the Waiters Union. But there have never been many people in the Waiters Union at any one time. We started with two or three households 20 years ago; there have rarely been more than 20 households at any one time during the network's journey. And those who are happy to be associated with us, may not generally be regarded as a "Waiters household."

The Waiters Union is not a high profile group locally. As Waiters, we try to keep a low profile in the area. None of the activities that we are involved in carry our name. They all carry the names of the groups who organise those activities, which we contribute to, but we do not control. As a result, a lot of people in our area may know us well as people, but may not even know that the group we are part of exists. Which is fine, because the group exists to promote the community, not the group; and the group can function more effectively as a catalyst in the community if it

---

[2] See "A Waiters Union Liturgy" in the End Notes.

The Network –
What is the Waiters Union?

is prepared to be more or less invisible, rather than attract attention to itself at the expense of other groups. However, we are not secretive. We welcome enquiries and answer questions as freely and as fully as we can. We aim to be inclusive. We invite anyone who is interested in our work to work with us as partners in the work together.

All the work we do is self-directed and other-orientated. We tend to work informally as individuals through existing networks. Whenever we choose to work formally as collectives we usually work together as a small group rather than a big organization. Being part of a group depends on participation. A person becomes a part of a group, not by jumping through any hoops, but simply by participating in the group.

Once a person is a part of the group, they have the right to manage the group they are a part of. We believe people should have the right to shape all the decisions that impact on their lives. We believe the best way for us to shape the decisions that impact on our lives, individually and collectively, is through the process of consensus.

So all the groups actually work *with* the people that they work *for* and, in so doing, seek to enable the people they work with, as *partners*, to realize their enormous potential as men and women made in the image of God.[3]

Monday mornings from 6.30 to 7.30 am we meet for worship, reflection and planning for the week. Throughout the week people meet in a range of groups to nurture their souls and sustain their faith and values. Every year different groups emerge to meet different needs and once those needs are met disappear as quickly as they appeared. However, year in, year out, on

---
[3] See "Waiters Union Activities" in the End Notes.

Sunday night from 6.30 to 8.00 pm we meet for public worship with local people in the basement of St Andrew's Anglican church.

Every two weeks we have a community meal, to which everyone is invited. Every six weeks we have a small gathering for fellowship with people in the network and every six weeks we have a large gathering with people in our region who are not in our network but who need continuing support for their faith-based community work.

Every six months we have a two-week live-in community orientation program which provides an intensive introduction or re-introduction to the spiritual disciplines that are the foundation for our faith-based community work. Every twelve months we have a camp, to give us the chance to get away and just relax together.

The most intensive learning experience found within the network is in a household dedicated to formation. Between four and six people live in this house at any one time. Many of the people in the network have spent time living in this more intense community household at one time or another. It serves as a resource for ongoing training in community development.

In 2010, groups helping Waiters explore spirituality, philosophy, politics, lifestyle and so on include short term study groups, a reading group, a documentary group, a men's group, and various groups focused on social justice issues. Some of these groups have been around for years, some are new, some might come to an end this year. All these meetings are managed by the people who participate in them, and while one person may act as contact across meetings, the facilitator role often changes.

One group of people the network is involved in has sought to promote the aspirations of the original inhabitants of our neighbourhood by lobbying for permission for them to build the as-yet-unbuilt cultural centre in Musgrave Park, which is in the middle of the neighbourhood.

Another group of people the network is involved in has sought to support refugees by sponsoring their settlement and the settlement of their families, working through the anguish they go through as "strangers in a strange land."

Through a whole range of groups in the network we have sought to relate to the people in our community who have physical, intellectual, and emotional disabilities – not as clients, nor as consumers, still less as users – but as our friends!

None of these things that any of us are doing seem that great. However, we constantly encourage one another to remember that true greatness is not in doing big things, but in doing little things with a lot of love over the long haul. And that is exactly what we are trying to do!

Dave Andrews and Helen Beazley (editors)

The Thing I Have Held Most Dear Through The Years
Angie Andrews

The thing I have held most dear through the years is
a vision of hospitality as a way of life.
It is a vision I have nurtured
in myself,
in my nuclear family
and in my extended family.
I believe it is the legacy of Jesus,
which I want to pass on
to my children
and to my children's children.

•

From 1973 to 1985
Dave and I lived in communities in Afghanistan and India.

These communities provided us with wonderful opportunities to learn how to live out a vision of hospitality in the vortex of chaos: comforting each other in our brokenness in the context of our battering, encouraging one another to find a way forward through our bewilderment.

I used to take refuge on the roof of our house every day.
I'd pray for God to give me the strength to live with the pain.
I'd turn for advice to my spiritual guide, who (at the time) was Mother Teresa. I'd read her writings, reflect on her words, and seek to "do God's will with a smile."

Ange is a follower of the nonviolent Jesus. She was raised in a Greek community and lived in an Indian community. She is married to Dave, with two daughters Vonnie and Navi, two sons-in-law Marty and Geyan, and two grandchildren Lila and Kaedin. She supports refugees in all aspects of settlement, creating employment options with marginalized groups.

Gradually our intentional communities grew into
therapeutic communities.

The addicts we met in drug dens,
the patients we visited at the hospital,
the prisoners we welcomed from the penitentiary
found their way to our house, found their way into our heart
and found there a place of healing.
And in their healing we found our healing.

•

In 1985
Dave and I returned to Australia.

We were determined to live in Australia
in the light of the lessons we had learnt in Afghanistan
and India.

We prayed that we could preserve our vision of hospitality
and reinterpret how we could live out the value of compassion
in this place.

I knew I could only start where I was with what I had.
Where I was – was in a neighbourhood with all these *wallahs*[4]
who were marginalized.
And what I had were all my *rels* [5] looking on to see what I was
going to do.

So with some forty first cousins in all watching over
my shoulder I began to write the next chapter of the history of
our family in this area. Had I given it a title at the time, I would
have called it "Inclusion."

I knew that if I was going to translate my experience

---

[4] "wallahs" is an affectionate Indian word for "people." It is one of Angie's favourite words.
[5] "rels" is short for "relatives." It is another one of Angie's favourite words.

*The Thing I Have Held Most Dear
Throughout the Years*

of hospitality in Afghanistan and India
into my community in Australia,
it would need to start with inclusion.

Inclusion was important for me,
because I had learnt that at the heart of hospitality was
compassion and that compassion with open arms always started
with inclusion.

So I began by including
the marginalized people I met in the neighbourhood
into the core of my family
by treating all the *wallahs* I befriended as my *rels*.

As you can imagine many of my rels
would stop me in the street and ask me:
"Angie why are you doing this?
You are a good girl, why are you hanging around with
these (bad) people?"

I would tell them that:
"They are not bad people. They are troubled people.
Because many of them have had bad things happen to
them in their lives. And you'd be troubled too, if the same
things had happened to you."

"Yes. Angie. That may be true.
But why should you be involved with them?
After all, you are a mother, with your own children
and you should be caring for your own children."

"That's exactly the point."
I would say.
"I believe God wants us

*The Thing I Have Held Most Dear
Throughout the Years*

to care for our children
and to teach them to care for others
just like their own relatives."

I was really happy
when my daughters Evonne and Navi
began to bring troubled people home.
I remember Evonne going out of her way
to befriend lonely kids at school
and bringing them home for me to meet
so we could talk with them
about how we could support them.

I remember Navi bringing home
a fourteen year old girl
who was pregnant.
She was under a lot of pressure
to abort her baby.
So we talked with her about her options.
And said that
if she wanted to keep her baby,
and needed a place to stay,
she was more than welcome to stay with us.

•

One of the basic rules in community work is:
never do on your own what you can do with others.

So when I began including
the marginalized people I met in the neighbourhood
into the core of my family
by treating all the *wallahs* I befriended as my *rels*,
I invited others to join me on my journey.

The Thing I Have Held Most Dear
Throughout the Years

A group of students
told me they were interested;
so we decided
to go on the journey together.

We used to meet at my house to
study a passage about the importance of inclusion
from a book I had by Mother Teresa,
remind ourselves of the people in our neighbourhood
who were forgotten
then visit a group living with disabilities in a hostel
run by Norma Spice in Russell Street West End.

One day I remember saying to these students
that if we were really going to relate to these *wallahs* as our *rels*
we needed to not only visit them in their hostels,
but also invite them back to our own homes.

The students said they were happy enough to visit people
in the hostels, but were afraid to invite people back to their
own homes. But I said to them, as followers of Jesus, we are
called to "not be afraid" –
to "not be afraid" to relate to these "brothers and sisters"
as our "family."

I knew one of the students was having a house warming party
that weekend. And I encouraged her to invite the hostel
wallahs as well as her other *rels*.
Eventually she decided to include them, and they had such a
great time that they became good friends and have stayed good
friends till today.

It was the beginning of a revolution of inclusion.

•

The Thing I Have Held Most Dear
Throughout the Years

As word went around about what we were doing
others asked to join us.
We would talk to them
about the legacy of Jesus,
about his vision of hospitality as a way of life,
about his call to be filled to overflowing with a spirit
of compassion.

We would specifically talk to them
about Jesus' challenge to include people in our parties
who were left off other people's party lists.

As a result of these discussions
we decided to host an open community meal
on a Friday night at someone's house every fortnight.

Right from the start we decided this would be
a shared meal
where everyone was encouraged to bring something to share,
rather than a soup kitchen
where everything was provided by someone else.

So right from the start there was an expectation
that not only would everyone be included
but also everyone would contribute.

Those who had more brought hot pots.
Those who had less brought tea bags.

And the tradition continues to this day.

What has changed over time is how people interact.

When we started the community meal
there was very little direct eye contact.

The Thing I Have Held Most Dear
Throughout the Years

People used to come in silence, with no smiles.
With their heads hung down, they would collect their meal
eat their meal without talking to anyone and leave as
quickly as they could.

Now, people arrive hours early and stay on as late as they can.
There is lots of hubbub as people greet each other and
give one another hugs.
There are still some people who choose to sit in silence;
but most people laugh and cry as they talk over their meal
about their week.
And most people are happy to pitch in with setting up, serving
and cleaning up.

•

Over the years it has become clear
that through the spirit that is at work within us
somehow or other, none of us knows how
we have discovered the power
to help one another and to heal one another.

One night when I was sick
Ted came to my house.
He stood outside in the dark.
I could not see him; but I could hear his voice;
saying he felt for me and he was praying for me.
It was as if an angel had come to comfort me.

Another night, when my brother died,
(after he had thrown himself off the Storey Bridge)
Dave was telling people about his death.
And Dean came up to Dave,
wrapped his arms around him and said:
"Don't worry Dave. I'll be your brother-in-law."

*The Thing I Have Held Most Dear
Throughout the Years*

When my (adopted) daughter Navi
(who was born in Nepal)
was being taunted by racist skinheads,
it was people from a nearby hostel
who came to her aid
and offered her their protection.

And when my daughter Evonne
decided to marry Marty,
she extended an open invitation
to all the people from the hostels.
Many of them attended the wedding
and some of them were in the wedding party.
The presence of these *wallahs*
together with the rest of our *rels*
was a small glimpse of heaven on earth.

•

I always wanted to be mindful of
those who were far away,
as well as those who were nearby.

When we bought a house,
we bought at the bottom end of the market
and decided to pay the mortgage off little by little
so we could set aside money to give to others overseas.

When Navi turned eighteen, she wanted to track down
her birth family.
We flew to Nepal and tracked down her sisters and
their families.
Two of the three sisters were very poor,
so we helped them buy small plots of land and build

The Thing I Have Held Most Dear
Throughout the Years

their own houses.

I wanted to welcome strangers, particularly refugees who came from far off lands
so I joined the Refugee Learning Centre in West End.

There I was able to meet refugees, welcome them to Australia, teach them English, talk with them one by one, listen to their stories, assess their needs and then find volunteers in the community who were happy to help them.

These volunteers eventually became known as the West End Refugee Support Group.
Twice a year for the last twenty years
I have taken a session in the Community Orientation course we run when I talk about the work of the West End Refugee Support Group.

I continually stress that the core role of our volunteers
is to use the opportunity of helping refugees
to be with them, befriend them and be faithful to them in their time of distress – dispossessed of country, property, family, friends and even their own identity.

Sara Parrott and Ewen Heathdale started a no-fees no-interest revolving loan scheme
to enable refugees with visas but no money to pay for their fares to Australia. About a hundred refugees have come through that scheme.
And there have been zero defaults on loan repayments.

Peter Westoby and Russell Eggins supported many refugees from Latin America: meeting arrivals at the airport and settling them in houses they found and furnished.

The Thing I Have Held Most Dear
Throughout the Years

We started a special torture and trauma support
group with them.
Waves upon waves of refugees came to Australia fleeing
war-torn regions: Indo China, Central Asia, South Asia and
The Horn of Africa.
So we started an interfaith dialogue group
for Christians, Buddhists, Hindus and Muslims to get
to know one another.

And the work goes on.
Recently I helped in a complex two-year refugee settlement
case, assisting the reunification of an Eritrean refugee
in Australia with her fiancé in a refugee camp in the Sudan.
Then I organised volunteers
to help her through her complicated pregnancy,
and subsequently arranged work for her and her husband.

But often there is no work
or the work that is there is not suitable
(for single parents who have lost their partners in wars
and need to work at home so they can supervise their children).
So Judy Collins-Haynes and I have negotiated contracts
for bulk orders of conference bags
then organized volunteers
to train refugee women to sew at a professional level
and to supervise the production of the conference bags
by the refugee women sewing in clusters at home.

Most of the work I have done
has been unfunded or has been underfunded.
So we have had to have to put on
lots and lots of fundraising events
to raise money for our work with refugees.

*The Thing I Have Held Most Dear
Throughout the Years*

And I've never been happier
than working alongside my daughters
putting on dinners for hundreds of people
to raise money to support refugees.

•

One of my most significant memories
was when Evonne and her husband Marty,
were living in the Bristol Street Household
with our younger daughter Navi,
their childhood friend Olivia,
and a couple of others.

The Bristol Street Household,
located on the main street of West End
was a place devoted to developing an everyday spirituality
that gladly put itself at the disposal
of the people who came to the door of their house
looking for help.

And they invited Dave and me to move in with them.

The next eighteen months
proved to be one of the best times of our lives.

We got on well.
We prayed together, laughed and cried together,
cooked and cleaned together, and grew together.

And I was able to see how my children
had grown into adults
and were now including their *rels*
into their lives,
along with all the other *wallahs*.

•

*The Thing I Have Held Most Dear
Throughout the Years*

It is my prayer
that all of us who have been involved in the network
(we now know as the Waiters Union)
will all find our own way
of living out our vision of hospitality in our community.

2010

A Ready Made Community Network
Steve Collins-Haynes

For me the Waiters Union has been a ready-made community network to connect with since 1987.

I got to know a couple of members of the network through a protest about rising rents around the time of the 1988 World Expo. Since then I've become friends with quite a few people in the Waiters Union and participated in many activities of the network.

Another big thing the Waiters Union has done for me has been to bring my wife, Judy, and I together. We met at a "community meal" one Friday night many years ago. We got to know each other as friends when we lived in the Bristol Street household. This household was committed to personal growth and justice in our neighbourhood and our world. Living in the Bristol Street household provided a great context to work on my own life and to establish a lasting relationship. Judy and I decided to get married after being friends for many months.

In my time of involvement with the Waiters Union I've had at least three major break-downs (some might say these were a result of my involvement). Seriously, though, these breakdowns have been long painful experiences for me and my family.

People from the Waiters Union have helped in many ways. Some have visited me regularly in and out of hospital. Some have supported my wife Judy through these times. A couple of people started a local Grow group which helped significantly

---

Steve was born in Coolah, mid western NSW. He works as a carpenter. He has lived in West End Brisbane for the last 22 years. He has been married to Judy for 19 years and has two teenage children Julia 17 and Christopher 14. His hobbies are tinkering, brewing beer, surfing, and making wooden furniture. He is currently 50 years old.

with my mental health. Another past member counseled Judy and I through one of my breakdowns.

Currently I'm part of a "men's group" which meets once a fortnight at my place. The group provides a safe space to express our trials and successes, to learn from one another and to offer and receive support. I also see a counselor from outside the network to help me gain more control over my life.

It was through the support of a couple of people in the Waiters Union that I've been able to create and sustain my self employment. I run a small carpentry business from home. Many of my customers are from the network.

The Waiters Union has been a great network to be involved in over the years I have lived in West End. I feel I've experienced a level of support that many people wish for. I feel privileged to be a part of it. I think it is quite unique.

It has made my life in West End incredibly rich.

2005

I Cannot See Myself Living Anywhere Else
Sannie Pritchard

In 1991 my youngest daughter interrupted her university studies to move into the Bristol Street household in West End, despite the fact that a few members of our local church questioned the wisdom of my allowing her to do so. "How can you? West End is such a dangerous place." During that year I sometimes came across on a Friday night to join in a share meal at the Thomas Street house which, of course, brought me into contact with a wide range of people, some of which I had never come across in my safe middle class suburbs.

In December 1991 I moved into the Thomas Street house for three weeks (yes, three weeks!) to be part of a Community Orientation Course. These three weeks blew my mind. Just being told to walk the streets and talk to people, the kind of people I had very seldom talked to before or spent time with. On the corner of Thomas and Vulture Street, where there has been a vacant space for many years now, there was a block of flats in which a number of Indigenous families lived. I can remember sitting on the footpath and spending time with the younger children. When we were told to find alternative accommodation for one of the three weeks, I joined forces with one of the younger women and eventually we found a room in a dilapidated house in Brighton Road. This has long gone. We had a bed and an old gas stove, which we never even tried. The bathroom was down the passage, a shower over the bath. The toilet was downstairs. Needless to say I never had anything to drink from the late afternoon, not wanting to go down the steps in the middle of the night!

When I went home after the course, disenchantment with the

Sannie grew up in South Africa; met Graham in London; married him in Brisbane; has four grandchildren; and likes exploring remote Australia.

local church deepened. Even before I had been tired of, for example, listening to excuses every week as to why someone could not possibly welcome at the door this Sunday. When I decided to work part-time, rent the house and move into a flat, one of four in a house in Brighton Road but more liveable than the previous one, I told people I was suffering from a mid-life crisis! So I plunged into the Waiters network. My memories are of the people and the things that were happening.

There were any number of younger, unmarried people and new household combinations were set up at different times. A new household usually had a housewarming party to which an open invitation was given through the weekly newsletter, parties where we danced the night away. At the Bristol Street house I had my first experience of such a party where people were dancing in a circle around the room to loud rock-and-roll music. I watched, as usual for me, but I was pulled in and it became a most liberating experience. Just to be able to move to the music, no concern about a partner, no concern about what I looked like, because everybody else was doing the same. I remember a 21st birthday party with an open invitation and a request to come in costume; even a few open invitation weddings.

It was as if I could not cope with everything people were involved in: helping mostly South American refugees to resettle, teaching English and befriending individual refugees, chicken co-ops, innumerable meetings about the possibility of buying a property near Coolum and what to do if it was bought, a finance co-op where each member contributed a small amount each month and you could get a small interest free loan if you required one, besides 6.00 am Monday morning meetings, 6.30 pm Sunday evening services, regular gatherings to worship together and catch up, picnics with friends in hostels, probably others I was not even aware of. Sunday evening services bring to mind the liturgies for which there was a roster, but for which there was no liturgy folder (however dilapidated!). Instead there was a bag with a few resource books and copies of previous liturgies. After the service the bag was passed on to the person who had to prepare a liturgy for the next Sunday. The most amazing and creative liturgies were regularly produced from a wide range of sources. I still have a few in a folder at home. Putting together a liturgy was one thing, but to stand up in front of everybody and lead the service, was quite another. Something which I found very difficult at first, but which I have grown to appreciate. Speaking at church was something I thought I would never do, could never do, but it happened. This I still find a very draining experience so I never rush to volunteer to have a turn to speak!

In Boundary Street there was also the Catholic Worker community house. On Tuesday nights after the evening meal they had an open liturgy. So I regularly went on a Tuesday night, usually bringing a contribution towards the meal. Just had to be careful to take my containers home, because what stayed behind became part of their household! Again the people. There was a woman with a baby who was being supported in caring for the baby with the long-term aim of her keeping the baby; there was an Indigenous man who would invite me for coffee if he saw me going past; there was Jim's mother who came to live and be cared for. I was even asked once to come and stay for a weekend and look after her. Between the Catholic Workers and the Waiters I was made aware of injustices both here and in other places. There were discussions about nonviolence, preparations for possible arrest, prayer times and vigils. I took part in rallies and marches and protests regarding Bougainville and East Timor, I went with groups to the Canungra Army Base to protest there. I became very interested in East Timor, reading widely for background information, volunteering to spend a day in the city doing a personal vigil. And now I'm involved in the West Papua Solidarity Group. Then there were Indigenous issues, both local and Australia wide. So I read and went to meetings and listened to people like Aunty Jean to become better informed; again, there were marches and rallies and still, every January, there is the Invasion Day gathering and march, and volunteering at the Family Fun Day held in Musgrave Park during NAIDOC week. After all this it seemed natural to join in the march to oppose the first Gulf War and to join silent vigils in King George Square in the lead up to the second. Injustice never seems to go away and support for just causes, however limited is ongoing.

There were also different forms of worship. The Christmas Eve midnight service at St Mary's Catholic Church in South Brisbane was always special, the music was glorious. There was a stations of the cross on the back of a ute with Catholic Workers and others, moving from one unethical company to another in the city and ending up at the abortion clinic in Bowen Hills. This started mid afternoon on the Thursday before Easter. Afterwards some were going to a service at St Mary's so I joined them and found, for the first time in my life, there was a cycle of Easter services from Thursday night to Sunday morning. I know I was waiting for the Thursday service to finish, it had not come to a close, there was darkness, but talking to others later I could understand that was how it should be as Jesus had gone out into the night to pray. My experience of Easter had always been an early service on Good Friday and the usual service on Sunday and in between you could do what you wanted to. Now I find myself unwilling to go away at Easter, sometimes looking for a church nearby that provides a full cycle, but sometimes staying with the local church's three hour service on Friday.

At Bristol Street there was Heretics Corner on a Friday morning where faith and Jesus and life were talked about and which opened so many windows. Having spent seven years of my life not doubting but actively hating God, it was such a relief to find that it was nothing to be ashamed of, that it was possible to doubt God. That we were all on different trajectories in relation to God, that we were not boxed in to a certain set of expectations.

In the beginning I went to a number of activities and meetings, but I sort of drifted towards the Friday picnics which I am still involved with though now only once a month and on a Saturday. For quite a few years a semi-retired couple and I arranged a picnic on alternate Fridays, each with friends from a different hostel. When they went on holiday and another bus driver had been found, I had to buy all the food for the picnic and only then realised how much it cost to keep the picnics going. After that I bought some of the provisions. The man died too many years ago; although now in her seventies and living in a retirement village, his wife was still coming to picnics in 2009. Meeting people in hostels and becoming friends of course exposed me to their lives and sometimes glimpses of their stories. I can remember being advised just to go to one of the hostels and visit people, which was a daunting prospect, but eventually I scraped up the courage to do so. As one hostel was closed and people moved to another place, I became aware of how controlled their lives were, how little independence they had, how badly they were sometimes treated. As I got to know a few better and became friends, it sometimes hurt to realise how little I could do to help them, I had to be content with being a friend.

When Flamingo Hostel closed a number of the people were moved to a place in Blakeney Street, a large house that had been built in underneath. Here there were a number of room groupings which each had a couple of bedrooms, a living space, a bathroom and a kitchen sink and fridge. This was really good for a while, I could visit and be offered a cup of tea, their meals were brought in so they could eat around their own table. This arrangement did not last long. Here I also, without really knowing what was happening, developed a deeper friendship with an older woman, Smithy. I can remember her coming to share meals, I have photos of her dancing at share meal parties, she used to come to picnics. Gradually, however, she withdrew. Why go to picnics? You only saw the same people! Fair enough. She liked to come out with me though, at first for a coffee, later for meals at my place. She never talked much but when she did I got snippets of her life, she had a son and a daughter but as far as I knew they never contacted her. There was one memorable day when I took her out for coffee, having a few days earlier been in to see her and arranging with the staff to take her out. As luck would have it, no-one was around when we left. By the time we got back they had discovered she was gone, had forgotten my arrangements, had already called the police and I was in serious trouble. All I could do was apologise because in the back of my mind was always the unspoken fear that if the manager took exception to anything I did or said, I would be refused entry. Smithy took this all in and later she said to me quietly "they forgot, didn't they?" After a move to yet another hostel, Smithy was moved to a place near Ipswich where I still went to visit and take her out for coffee until she died. When I prepared for her funeral I realised that, during years when my life had been difficult, she had given me some stability, had been an anchor, someone I could go and visit and have a coffee with.

With picnic groups we have travelled far and wide, even as far as Bribie Island and once to Coochiemudlo Island! Over the years we have developed our favourite picnic spots, like Bellbird Grove and Shorncliffe, but we always keep a look out for new places. We know which are the best places to go if it looks like rain, or is raining. Rain does not stop us! We have been known to cook the sausages under an umbrella.

When a friend who was also involved with picnics discovered free ABC concerts in Ferry Road, Hill End on Sundays we regularly took a bus full of hostel friends to these. We also attended some of the Lord Mayor's free music concerts in the City Hall. Both myself and my friends were all younger and possibly more adventurous! One December a bus load of us went to look at the Christmas lights in the Kenmore area.

Coming into the Waiters network I think I saw people and how they were living out their faith through rose coloured glasses, to me they were just so special. So it took a while to accept that the network of people was just a microcosm of the larger society in as much as some were born, some died, some were married and some were divorced. I know I found even the thought of the first two divorces difficult to cope with, especially as I was in a home group with one couple. As well, there were disagreements among various members of the network, of which some were not resolved. There were people who left for this reason. There were also people who left because they were disillusioned, because they had not found what they had imagined from reading some of the books about the network. There were some who drifted to the edges but still stay involved with friends they had made. Over the years this has been balanced, for me, by couples who have stayed together and supported each other through incredibly difficult situations, and who are still doing so –

by people who are still prepared to go with their friends on picnics, even as the groups get smaller and smaller. People who have shared at times their vulnerability either speaking at church or in the gatherings. People who have journeyed with me, who were willing to listen to me when I felt vulnerable; when I wondered if there was something the matter with me after I had been exposed, for example, to some of the faith ideas of family members. People who showed me how to live my faith in practical ways, which was good, because I am more of a practical person. Like sharing a car for 10 years, like growing vegetables, like more recently going on a carbon fast and trying a local diet for two weeks, like installing PV panels on my roof. People who have become friends and who will listen to me when I just want to talk! Living on my own and having been an "alone" person all my life, this is particularly precious.

Having started this I feel there is so much more, but ... impossible to go on and on. I do not live in West End any more, having bought in Highgate Hill in 1998, but I still hang around. So I have grown old within the Waiters network and I have come to accept both myself and the fact that we are all human with each having our strengths and weaknesses. I have to accept, sometimes reluctantly, that I get tired and do not have the same energy levels and this limits my commitments. I am encouraged by the fact that a number of younger people have moved into the network in recent years and are connecting as well as doing their own experimenting.

Although there are no other people my age within the network, I sort of cannot see myself living anywhere else.

2010

A Local's Evaluation Of The Waiters Union
Stephanie Becker

My first contact with the Waiters Union had been through church meetings that are held every Sunday night at 6.30 pm in St Andrews Anglican Church South Brisbane. I visited those meetings on several occasions, without really knowing about the Waiters Union. To learn more I read *Christi-Anarchy* and *Building a Better World*, conducted internet research, visited a Waiters gathering, community meal, and the Monday morning meeting. I also talked to some people associated with the Waiters Union.

To write a paper in the true modernist sense about the Waiters Union seems a contradiction in itself, since the people who see themselves connected to the Waiters Union avoid naming, classifying or structuring their idea of life, relationships and friendships together. Even the term "community" does not fit the Waiters Union, as it is a group of people who strive to live towards community – it is a dynamic process rather than a static construct. The persons in the Waiters Union are deliberately avoiding structures, programs or set agendas, they are instead a bunch of people who aim to be simply present and available for one another.

West End seems the ideal place for the Waiters as it is located in the bend of the Brisbane River and even though it is very close to the inner city, it has a more village-like feel to it, and it has a different pace to the rest of Brisbane. West End is a densely populated suburb, with a high percentage of low-income households (even though that is dramatically changing) as well as a

---

Stephanie was born in 1972 in Germany and moved to Australia in 1999. She moved to West End in 2000 where she is currently living with her husband and two children. Stephanie works as an acupuncturist, counsellor and natural therapist.

high migrant population. Waiters see themselves not apart from the locality, but as a part of the locality and as a network of residents who work towards community that is integral to the locality.

The Waiters Union is inclusive of everybody, regardless of race, gender, sexuality or religion. The Waiters aim to reflect the love of Christ, to develop a relationship to Christ and relationships to people through Christ. Some make a clear distinction between a Christian and someone who is aiming to be Christ-like.

The Waiters Union can appear to be rather fuzzy, undefined and hard to grasp, for our structuralist mindset. However, this absence of structure makes it inclusive of all people, faiths and life circumstances. There are no clear determining indicators of who is in or out, because there is no defined membership. Unlike some other traditional Christian communities, the Waiters adopt a Christ-centred approach where people are seen as constantly moving towards Christ, instead of being boxed into a mould which makes them either Christians or non-Christians, insiders or outsiders, saved or unsaved.

Inclusive conversation and communication is at the heart of the Waiters Union, which invites everybody to participate or contribute with the gifts they have. Through conversation (which is closely related to the word *conversion*), Christ as a figure can be found in *any* human story regardless of religion. The Christ Story runs deeply through a human's heart.

The Waiters are an intentional community of people who have a common idea about the neighbourhood, social justice and the role of Christ in their lives. In some sense, the Waiters Union is a transformative community, despite its deliberately low profile.

Dave Andrews says, "Change may start with us, but if it stops with us it will stop altogether; we need to make changes, but others need to make changes too."

Like Jesus, the Waiters see themselves as servants to their neighbourhood offering help, hospitality and a desire to listen to people's stories, understand their problems and work towards solutions. They do not seek to establish power hierarchies and structures but engage in social justice and peaceful resistance. The focus is on building relationships as well as on issues in the immediate neighbourhood regarding Indigenous groups, refugees, people with drug addictions, people in boarding houses, people with a mental illness, or otherwise marginalised neighbours.

Like Jesus who criticised institutionalised religion and oppressive power structures, the Waiters deliberately choose to avoid the pitfalls of institutionalisation, because of the tendency of institutions to dehumanise individuals, and people are easily reduced to labels. One of the precautions to avoid hierarchy is the chosen flat structure. Any person can become part of the Waiters Union, and everyone can participate in decision making within the Waiters Union.

The lack of structure promotes mutual accountability rather than hierarchical accountability. Even though Dave is a prominent figure in the Waiters Union he sees his role as a facilitator not an initiator, he aims to enable people instead of taking charge in a leadership role. He aims to relate to all people as equals.

This seems to be a struggle at times because people are used to the prevalent paradigm of leadership and subordinates and frequently refer back to him for answers. This thought has been confirmed in a conversation with a woman who used to be with the Waiters but moved away. She said that if there were problems, people would refer back to Dave.

That does not mean that I disagree with the idea of a flat structure, I simply believe that it is difficult to maintain the view that there is no traditional leadership role amongst the Waiters. It is a given that some people have greater leadership qualities than others. It is a matter of how leadership is conducted. Jesus had a leadership role, yet he did not exert power over people in an oppressive sense, he enabled people, he encouraged people and created awareness of their freedom. In that sense, it might be a question of redefining leadership, instead of rejecting it.

The neighbourhood plays an important role in the Waiters Union. For many people in the area who lack the mobility to leave their neighbourhood this is important. This focus on the neighbourhood is coherent with Jesus' desire that we ought to love our neighbour and if we lack interaction with our neighbour, we miss what Jesus has asked us to do. This is a strongly counter-cultural push in an increasingly fragmented society in which the poorest and most marginalised suffer the most. To live in a neighbourly way of helping, listening and being present with the other seems to be almost a radically new thought.

The ministry of the Waiters is diverse and they have various projects or activities, which create a deepening of relationships and community. They are committed to meeting each other's needs. In addition, the way in which some of the members contribute their gifts, money or other possessions, work in unpaid jobs as well as pooling resources creates to my understanding a resemblance of Acts 2 and 4. This is the "visionary agenda of Jesus of Nazareth" – to choose poverty over wealth, hardship over comfort, commitment to availability to everyone at the cost of one's own privacy, to serve everyone. But Jesus also retreated on a mountain to have refuge from people and to spend time only with God. Jesus also fled the crowd to be alone with his disciples. I believe "unlimited" availability to the other is not biblical and not healthy and would lead to burn out, if it is not balanced with time alone and time with God.

The ministry is evident in different groups and anyone can start a new group. There are groups doing a range of activities, a men's and a women's group, world music gatherings, support groups for refugees, community meals, a church service, Monday morning meetings to sing, meditate, reflect and discuss issues, and many more initiatives. An incorporated association with strong links to the Waiters can provide assistance to those seeking grants for their groups or needing legal cover. It acts in a servant nature – from below – having Jesus as an example.

An important gathering for the Waiters is the 6.30 pm service on Sunday nights. I went to this service, which is at times referred to as "chaos" church in an endearing sense. The services are open to everyone and many people from the area who live in boarding houses and hostels, and are mentally or intellectually challenged or otherwise marginalised, find a place here to be together, chat, pray, laugh, cry, share joys and worries, find an ear and share a warm cup of coffee and a biscuit with friends.

The service is as non-structured and non-hierarchical as possible, anybody can give a talk if they want to and no one person dominates. Unlike most churches where the congregation faces each other's back and towards an "elevated" minister or a transcendent God, the Waiters have arranged circles. I feel this is more like how Jesus would have sat with his disciples, facing each other. A circle is inviting and inclusive. When I participate in a service, I become aware of how authentic it is. No one carries a social mask, the service and the people are stripped of pretension and social codes of conduct. When we sit in the circle, we are equal, all broken in some way.

I sense that Jesus is right amongst us with all our imperfections, indeed it feels as if these are the people Jesus would be sitting with, the people who are normally excluded from clean and proper church meetings, the ones with very little power, the ones who have time and are never too busy. It is certainly counter-cultural and that is exactly what Jesus was. He did not accommodate the norm, he was critical of the leadership and the masses. Another important aspect is that it is a forum to discuss Indigenous and social justice events. That means the gathering does not stop at the church doors. It also highlights that faith is connected to social action and concern for the other and not simply a religious exercise.

I also appreciate the simplicity of the service itself. No ecstatic music team, no overly joyous leadership trying to convince the audience that all suffering is overcome. This service creates room for a God who is evident and experienced in suffering. He is not just the King of Glory in shining armour promising earthly riches but he is also a God who can be found through suffering and in suffering.

However, I believe a danger is that the Waiters can become self-righteous. Because the message is in stark contrast to what mainstream society is living, there is a danger of becoming judgmental towards the ones who live a different way of Christianity.

I remember that some years ago, I met someone whom I now know is part of the Waiters. I asked her if she attended a church and her reply indicated that she did, but in a different way from other Christians. Her answer and demeanour demonstrated to me disrespect for others. I believe there is a danger of falling into a similar trap as some other congregations do, namely to be better than the other.

A core group of the Waiters meets on Monday mornings at 6.30 am. When I visited we were seven people, singing and reading out of a book before reflecting on it. What struck me was the honesty with which we could discuss and reflect on questions without threatening someone's theology. I assume because Jesus stands above religion and theology it is possible to ask questions. Again we sat in a circle and sang. A beautiful way to start a week.

To me it seems the Waiters open windows for other voices to be heard, they try to live the message of Jesus not in a Christian, but in a Christ-centred way, focusing on Christ's life and actions and discovering that his message is very much in contrast with the cultural paradigms, and it offers an inclusive message for the ones that otherwise would have little value in society.

Personally, I have been very touched by the vision of the Waiters. I feel deep within myself that the approach of a Christ-centred, non-structural, non-institutionalised, non-religious, non-hierarchical way of living together and helping each other out, and having a heart and the will to confront the injustice that occurs globally and locally is deeply at the centre of the message of Jesus.

2003

Training
What training do people in the Waiters Union provide?

Like many things to do with the Waiters Union it is often hard to figure out where the training starts and ends. Everyone would agree that most of the training provided by people in the Waiters Union occurs informally as an integral unpaid part of their ordinary everyday life – a process Ange describes beautifully in "The Thing I Have Held Most Dear Through the Years."

Shortly after Dave and Ange returned to Australia, they were both hired by Baptist Community Services. Ange was hired to do community work with women and children at risk, and later to do community work specifically with women and children from refugee backgrounds; while Dave was hired to provide training in faith based community work.

Over time Dave and Ange negotiated to do much of their work in the context of the Waiters Union that was emerging in West End. Their hope was that West End in general and the Waiters Union in particular, would provide a helpful context for training in faith-based community work focused on work with vulnerable groups of people.[6]

•

These days the Training Team operates as a program of the Community Initiatives Resource Association ("the Resource

---

[6] Dave negotiated to share his part time salary with others from the Waiters Union in order to include more people from the Waiters Union in the provision of the training. And since then a succession of people from the Waiters Union have been employed by Baptist Community Services – and later the Community Initiatives Resource Association supported by the Vision for Mission team of the Uniting Church in Australia – in the provision of training: including Neil Barringham, Mark Blum, Judy Collins-Haynes, Thomas Day, Gerard Dowling, Karen Drimer, Neil Hockey, Greg Manning, Ian Morris, Jenny Nash, Christel Palmer, Chris Todd, Evonne Richards, Marty Richards and Peter Westoby. That fact notwithstanding, it needs to be understood that much of the training provided by many of the people in the Waiters Union (including all the people who have been named) is being provided for little payment, low payment, or no payment at all.

Association"), offering seven training options.[7]

1. Community Work Talks (one hour)
Preliminary presentations on the characteristics of Christ's call to incarnate the gospel in our own communities.

2. Community Work Workshops (one day)
Preparatory seminars on the basic spiritual, personal and relational dynamics of Christ-like community work.

3. Community Orientation Courses (two weeks)
An intensive course held in West End, Brisbane mid year (June/July) and again at the end of the year (early December). The course is a two-week, grass-roots, face-to-face, show-and-tell, do-it-and-discuss-it introduction to Christ–centred community work. There are a range of inputs from people involved with Indigenous Australians refugees and people with disabilities in the neighbourhood, as well as people experimenting with alternative initiatives based on fair trade, inclusion, co-operation, nonviolence and sustainability. Most of the time participants live in a joint household, but stay overnight now and then with people in the community. The course includes personal reflection, interpersonal interaction, group process, cooperative organisation, whole hearted, holistic engagement, cross cultural communication, inter–faith dialogue, practical service and non-violent action.

4. Community Work Placements (three months)
An opportunity for people who want an introductory experience of community work in general and Christ-centred community work with the poor in particular. It involves living in

---

[7] See "The Community Initiatives Resource Association" in the End Notes.

a supervised community household and being involved in a range of community activities. Mostly university and seminary students looking for faith-based community work placements take up this training option.

5. Community Work Internship (six to twelve months)
An opportunity for people who want an advanced experience of community work in general, and Christ-centred community work with the poor in particular. It involves living in a supervised community household and being involved in a range of community activities. Usually members of the household do not work or study full time so that they have more time to connect with and support people and groups in the community.

6. Faith-Based Community Work Course (from one session to two semesters)
This course addresses two units of competency from the Community Services Training Package. The first unit focuses on support for community participation. And the second unit focuses on support for community leadership. It is delivered flexibly by extension throughout Australia through the Australian College Of Ministries and as a unit called "Building Community" at Trinity College.

7. Project Hope (half a day every six weeks)
Project Hope seeks to encourage faith-based community workers to integrate Christian faith and community life. Some of its key concerns are: helping participants develop a healthy balance between their inner and outer lives – a congruence between their personal spirituality and their public activities; challenging people to move out of theirs obsessions with "self" and into practical "others-orientated" Christianity; and encouraging people to think of how they can sustain themselves

long term in the service of Christ rather than being crippled by discouragement. Project Hope meetings are characterised by interactions with people around South East Queensland and Northern New South Wales who share their experience of grappling with the complexities of life with Christ in their localities.

•

Dave Andrews and Chris Todd, who originally developed the training, often talked about the *inner dimension* of the training as well as the *outer dimension* of the training or what they called the *soul* of the training that was embodied in these seven training options. They described the *soul* of the training as *in-situ, spiritual, experiential, personal, relational, ethical, action-reflection* community development education that was *transformational*.

In-situ training

A lot of community development training is usually conducted in the context of an *agency*, while our community development training is conducted in the context of the *community*. Our *in-situ* training, is provided in the context of West End, and in the context of the West End Waiters Union. (The Community Praxis Co-op – which grew out of the Waiters Union provides similar training.) [8]

Spiritual training

This training seeks to provide people with the opportunity to explore a dynamic *spirituality* that is essential for developing a healthy community. In our training we often express this as the *Trinity* being the *model*, the *Christ* being the *example*, the *Gospel* being the *process*, and the *Spirit* being the *power* for any healthy community development, especially faith-based community development.

---
[8] See "The Community Praxis Co-Op" in the End Notes.

Experiential training

This training seeks to provide the opportunity for people to *experience the sentiment*, the *sense of significance and solidarity*, at the *heart of community*. This training also seeks to provide an opportunity to experience the training as an experience of learning to develop *deep mutual respect* for one another, as in a *healthy extended family*.

Personal training

Community development is a *personal* issue – *it begins with us!* Either we can *complain* about the way things are, or we can *change* the way things are, *starting* with ourselves. This training provided by the Waiters Union gives people that start.

Relational training

Community development is a *personal* issue and a *relational* issue. *Change may start with us, but if it stops with us – it will stop altogether!* Our training helps people to help one another make the needed changes together.

Ethical training

Community development is at heart an essentially *ethical* activity. There are no short cuts. There are no quick fixes. The training stresses the fact that we cannot develop community unless we *do unto others as we would have them do unto us*.

Action-reflection training

We encourage people to remember that anything that is good enough to do is worth doing badly to begin with; but, if we want to do good, then each time we have a go at something, we should try to do it better than we did before. This means we all need to develop the capacity to *reflect critically on our actions*.

•

It has always been hoped that the in-situ, spiritual, experiential, personal, relational, ethical, action-reflection training could be *transformational*.

Some time ago, as part of a reform process started as a result of the famous Fitzgerald Inquiry into police corruption in Queensland, there was a renewed interest in transformational training. Training that would not only discuss and debate issues of personal integrity and social justice but also actually develop a commitment to personal integrity and social justice. However, though it is easy to teach about personal integrity and social justice in the classroom, it is difficult – if not impossible – to actually learn personal integrity and social justice anywhere but in the context of the ebb and flow of ordinary everyday life in the community itself.

We invite people to come and live with us in our community in the hope we can all learn something more about personal integrity and social justice. We introduce people to Aunty Jean, an Aboriginal leader who not only tells them the story of her people and their painful dispossession, but also takes them with her to meet her people, some in a maximum security prison, languishing in their cells, and others in a human rights organisation, fighting for their release. And we introduce them to Father Kefle, an Eritrean priest, who shows them the scars of 30 years of civil war, and they visit refugees who have been torn away from their families, tortured by the very people who were supposed to protect them, forced to flee for their lives, and are now struggling to rebuild a life for themselves as strangers in a strange land.

Some people have never actually met an Indigenous person or a refugee face to face before; let alone heard their story, or seen their struggle for themselves. These encounters confront people with questions that everyone has to answer one way or another.

1. "How do we, as members of a 'white' society deal with our 'black' history?"

2. "How do we, as members of the human family, respond to the desperate plea from our brothers and sisters, not just to address the superficial symptoms, but the underlying causes of their ongoing pain?"

3. "And what do you – and I – imagine that Christ would want us to do about it?"

These are questions which call for answers. Not merely theoretical answers. But practical answers. Answering these questions is a moral imperative that people can accept or reject, but which they cannot ignore.

One person at a course we ran, who accepted the moral imperative to answer these questions, as honestly as he could, was a cop we'll call Brad who had been on the beat for many years.

Brad said that, like a lot of police, who onlo ever related to people in their job as sources of information about "criminals," or as potential or actual "criminals" themselves, he had become quite cynical about the public. But, when he took the opportunity to get out of uniform, and to meet people he'd stereotyped, face to face, as fellow human beings, he began to change.

The first stage of change was in terms of *perspective*. What people see depends on where they stand. And standing with the very people he had often been expected to take a stand against, helped Brad see a different side to the struggle on the streets than the one he'd seen before.

The second stage of change was in terms of *responsibility*. What people hear depends on whom they listen to. And listening to people who he and his fellow officers didn't normally listen to helped Brad not only hear a different side to the story of the history of our society than the one he'd heard before, but also accept his part as a police officer in perpetuating that history.

The third stage of change was in terms of *pain*. How people feel depends on what they do. And recognising that what he was doing as a police officer was often part of the problem, rather than part of the solution, helped Brad feel the impact of the issues much more acutely than he'd ever felt them before.

The fourth stage of change was in terms of *responsiveness*. People have two options for managing the pain that comes from recognising the gap between who they are and who they are meant to be. One option is rationalisation – changing the ideal, so it is closer to who they are. The other option is transformation – changing the reality, so they are closer to becoming the person Christ wants them to be. The chance for Brad to choose transformation rather than rationalisation came along one day quite unceremoniously when a local murri [9] asked him for a smoke. Instead of moving on – as he usually did – this time Brad chose to stop, and have a smoke and a bit of a chat – like he would have done with any of his other mates. This small change was a big deal for Brad. Brad was at this stage when he completed the community orientation course.

He still had another stage to go.
The fifth stage of change is in terms of *practice*. People are what they do repeatedly. The transformation we seek in our lives –

---
[9] Indigenous people from most of present day Queensland are known as Murri.

and in the lives of those whom we train – is not an act, but the *habitual practice of a more Christ-like life of personal integrity and social justice.*

Dave Andrews and Helen Beazley (editors)

An Open Letter About the Input
Ashley Withers

The Gateway Centre
1052 Mt Gravatt Capalaba Road
MacKenzie Queensland Australia 4156

11th August 2005

To Whom It May Concern

On behalf of Gateway Baptist I wish to express my appreciation of the input we received from the Waiters Union.

The experience that the Waiters Union has developed through two decades of urban ministry has been helpful to those of us who are more recently endeavouring to engage with marginalised peoples.

At Gateway we have benefited on many occasions from their willingness to share their insights with us. Most recently we have gained from their experience in refugee support.

Two years ago at Gateway we began to explore the possibilities of having a ministry to refugees.

After initial discussions about beginning such a ministry, Dave and Ange Andrews met with a group of interested Gateway people on a couple of occasions to discuss the social, cultural and theological implications of working with displaced people who have come to Australia seeking refuge.

Ashley was born in Brisbane in 1960. He is very happily married to Paula, with two grown up children, Tirzah and Jason. Ashley and Paula served in missions in Central America and the Philippines between 1984 and 1997. Since 2003 Ashley has worked as the missions pastor and psychologist at Gateway Baptist Church in Brisbane.

An Open Letter About the Input

Dave and Ange gave invaluable input into the development of our refugee ministry and introduced us to Ewen Heathdale who spent many hours training our group and assisting us in establishing a good process for addressing the needs of new arrivals.

Through Ewen we were able to join the Community Support for Refugees program and over the last two years Ewen has tracked with us as we helped seven families and two single men to settle in Brisbane.

Marty Richards also met with our refugee group, at West End and at Gateway, to talk about issues affecting refugees in general and to explore avenues of support for Temporary Protection Visa holders.

We have consistently found the personnel of the Waiters Union to be available and open to help the Gateway Refugee Interest Group to find ways of getting involved.

I think that one of the greatest benefits that Baptist churches like ours gain from the Waiters Union is having a reference point to turn to when God prompts us to move beyond our comfort zones in ministry. Reaching out to marginalised people is God's heart, but for many of us in middle class suburbia this is unchartered territory.

Having access to people like Dave, Ange, Ewen and Marty has enabled us to step out with confidence, knowing that others who have been doing this kind of ministry for years are prepared to walk this journey with us.

Ashley Withers
Missions Pastor at Gateway

2005

Personal Reflections On The Experience
John Dacey

Raw, authentic, generous. These are some of the words that come to my mind when I pause to recall my time at the Waiters Union Community Orientation Course, December 2007.

It was raw in the best sense. Unprocessed, untreated, pure, organic even. Like we're told the best food for us is that which is organic and unprocessed, this Course was that. I could feel this Course doing me good as it was going down. Only this was food for the spirit; though the body didn't miss out either, with creative people in our group dishing up delectable meals from incongruous ingredients.

That incongruity was matched by the participants themselves: seventeen people from all walks, denominational affiliations, jobs, ages, life situations, nationalities, and theologies. We were all on different points of the spectrum (some of us even on different spectrums!). But something drew us all to this single point of seeking an authentic experience of the Christian life.

And authenticity is what we got. There's no pretence, no effort to put on a mask or try to show a face other than that which is the normal and everyday. Sure, we were an occasional intrusion into Waiters normality, but you quickly got the sense that their normality is totally geared towards accepting the traveler, the sojourner, the outsider. This, we discovered, is at the heart of community.

It was generous too. A "big" experience, not half-hearted or sparse, even though there was enough spare time to get ourselves

---

John is a Uniting Church Deacon who has worked ecumenically for social justice, community development, nonviolence and social change. John's current work is as Community Minister and Team Leader of a community development based ministry in Mt Druitt, a disadvantaged and multicultural area of western Sydney.

into trouble. But that is how we learned, by using the "spare" time to throw ourselves into an experience and see what came. We were treated as adults and encouraged to pursue our own learnings, with opportunities on offer including serving in soup kitchens, sleeping on the streets and accompanying hostel residents on a day out. There were plenty of times to talk with those we met on the streets, other Course participants and the many visitors and members of the Waiters Union who dropped in from time-to-time.

Overall, there was a wealth of experience of making Christian faith a reality among the down-trodden of society. Some amazing stories were shared of lives full of struggle with mental illness and victory over restrictive social structures and cultural prejudices. Through these and other stories, we built a picture of the significant impact that the activities of the Waiters Union have on those they serve. Together, they became inspiration for our own efforts which we were all better equipped to continue when we returned home.

Alongside the experiences and stories came conceptual frameworks, which wove together community development and theology into a seamless whole. Mysterious theological concepts such as the Trinity were made accessible and relevant by grounding them in the task of creating community in this individualistic world.

Community development wasn't restricted to the world of interpersonal relationships either; the sometimes hidden but nonetheless real structures of society which inhibit community were exposed and explored for ways to transform them.

It became clear that we weren't there to just consider that there is a different way of understanding reality, but to be equipped to be agents of change within our contexts to bring about the gospel mandate of what Jesus called the "reign of God", and what Martin Luther King Jr called "God's beloved community".

The Course gave me hope grounded in possibility. This thing called community is possible, not just some idealistic and hence unrealistic dream, but an achievable reality with guides and signposts to its realisation.

The Course was offered so subtly, so naturally that I found myself forgetting at times to apply myself to it to ensure that I got the most out of it I possibly could. It quickly became normalised, as if this is the way life was meant to be, not like doing a Course at all. If this is the intention, that participants be immersed in developing community so that they experience it as normal, then it worked for me, and left me wanting more.

This, of course, has consequences which are felt on returning home to so called normality. I think "culture shock" is the common name given to the things I felt when I got back to "reality". This is not to criticise the Course but to indicate its significance, such that I felt a "shock" on returning home.

We create our own realities and, the Course having created a reality for me called community, I'm more able to create that same reality in the contexts in which I find myself.

2008

Why We Send Our Staff For Training
Diane and Ross Coleman

Urban ministry among the poor and marginalised has been an interest of ours for many decades. Our initial exposure was through being involved with Baptist Inner City Ministries in inner city Sydney. Ross was involved in this ministry for many years as was I to a lesser extent. Our ministry involvement over the years since then has included prison work, working with the unemployed, counseling and church planting.

Incarnational mission and being "Jesus" to people who you live and work amongst has been a priority for our work. Therefore as we moved back to the inner city to live and work among the urban poor we sought to find others who had trod this path before us to learn from their experience as well as their theologising about what they were doing.

Our choice to attend the Waiters Union course was quite intentional: we wanted to explore the above with people who had been living and working in this environment for many years. Our experience of the structure of the course, living in community in West End and being part of the work there reaffirmed our thoughts for our own ministry in inner city Sydney.

Many from HOPESTREET Urban Compassion have attended the Waiters Union course. Indeed it is compulsory for our staff to attend this or a similar course as part of their ongoing work in Sydney. There are few options available in Australia where

---

Diane and Ross both work for Baptist Community Services. Diane is the manager of their counselling centre in Bankstown while Ross manages a community centre in Warilla. They enjoy the outdoors and have completed a number of long treks around the country. This is their time of regaining some sanity from the pressures of work and life. They have two children and two fantastic adorable grandchildren (slightly biased of course) who live with them. So their household is noisy at times. They are currently connected with HopeStreet Darlinghurst which seeks to engage authentically with people on the margins.

people can explore missional contexts especially among the marginalised where people are willing to live among the people they are reaching out to.

The Waiters Union provides a theological space to explore these issues with people who are willing to wrestle with and work through these issues and not come up with pat or easy answers. It has been heartening to find others who are continually exploring ways of being "Jesus" in these contexts where society generally disregards people as not worth the effort because they cannot rise above their current circumstances. Being "Jesus" in places where there is no "upward lift" due to poverty provides many challenges for ministry with sustainability being a constant challenge.

I believe that the Waiters Union provides a prophetic voice to the church and society so that all people regardless of whether they can pay or not can hear the voice of Jesus in their situation. The "inkind" love, support and friendship provided through people associated with the Waiters Union in West End challenges the most loving and giving of middle class churches that we have ever been part of.

2005

Learnings
What learnings do people derive from the Waiters Union?

We often get a lot of positive feedback from people about the workshops that we run. For example, 80% of the participants in a workshop we ran for the agency Liveability said that the training was excellent in terms of its relevance to their situation. Brent Clark's comment was typical: *"The best most relevant teaching about 'my situation' I have heard in years. Beautiful, man, beautiful."* But what is even more encouraging for us is the feedback we get about the space the training creates for people to do their own learning. Connie Gillett, who attended the Liveability workshop along with Brent Clark, said: *"I really loved it. (It was) very innovative and liberating – and allowed people to explore things within their own context."*

•

A few years ago we did a survey of people who had attended our Community Orientation Course, lived in our intentional community households and participated in our Project Hope circle of support, to assess what learnings people had derived from these training options.

Over 90% of respondents indicated they had learnt significant or highly significant lessons about community from attending a community orientation course – and over 70% reported they had learnt significant or highly significant lessons about care, service and non-violence (Andrews and Beazley *Jesus In The Neighbourhood* Brisbane 2005, p115).

> *I think the course gave me more of a "community consciousness." I value community a lot more and look for opportunities to be part of it. I tend to feel things are not just up to me to make better but I can just be part of the solution. I am happy for it all to feel pretty ordinary as*

Learnings – What learnings do people derive from the Waiters Union?

> *you just deal with the stuff of life (p119).*

> *The course has given me a glance at how I feel life is meant to be. Through participating with a community that was committed to seeking love, compassion and life, I was thoroughly challenged ... My life has changed dramatically as a result (p129).*

> *The emphasis on "voluntary" involvement (what I understand as being an exercise of "civil society") as opposed a "professional" approach, continues to be very influenttial (p119).*

> *The sessions on nonviolence were a huge gift to me – they gave me a way of understanding how to create change without being forceful (p121).*

Over 88% of respondents indicated they had learnt significant or highly significant lessons about *living and working with people in community* from living and working in an intentional community household – reporting significant or highly significant lessons about *working with people with disabilities, with people from refugee backgrounds* and *Indigenous people (p146)*.

> *I remember right from the start, on the first day of my placement, they really made me feel welcome. I felt a deep sense of belonging the minute I set foot on the front steps. Here I met Karen who made me a cup of tea and told me to make myself at home.*

> *One of the things that really stood out to me was the running of the household. People are given the opportunity to be themselves, and are able to express themselves in their own way. There is mutual respect between the*

people who live (in the house). People are actually concerned with the wellbeing of one another. For example, one of the members of the household is a vegetarian. Therefore those whose turn it is to cook always try to take her into consideration. The cook will prepare a special vegetarian dish especially for her. Another member is a reformed alcoholic. So the others are careful not to bring any alcoholic beverages onto the premises and visitors are asked not to do so either. One of the girls informed me that whenever she goes out to a party with this particular person, she won't drink any alcohol while she is with her.

The (people in the house) also treat others with the same type of respect, especially the large number of people with psychiatric disabilities who visit the place. Members of the household will often spend hours just sitting and talking to these people, listening to their stories. They make cups of tea for them, serve them lunch, and even take them out on social outings, a picnic, a barbecue, or a movie of their choice. Now if this isn't respect for the wellbeing of your neighbour, then what is it? (p58).

I grew during my time (there) as I had never grown before, but boy it hurt at times (p142).

I learnt that living in a community that tries to embody Jesus' love for others is hard work and often very painful (p142).

I discovered ways of living and relating that felt congruent with my faith; I felt loved and supported in ways I had never before experienced; I experienced pain of an intensity I had never before experienced; I touched the

> *lives of the poor and became friends through crossing cultural, socio-economic and racial divides. My time there (in the household) launched me on the course that my life has travelled (ever since) (p139).*

Over 80% of respondents indicated they had learnt significant or highly significant lessons about *community and mission* from participating in our project hope circle of support – reporting significant or highly significant lessons about *more sensitive ways of relating to others and more authentic, articulate and reciprocal ways of sharing their faith with others (p136).*

> *(Project Hope) has the ability to encourage, equip and empower others – from volunteers to ministers and leaders in management – to continue being involved in working to assist others (p72).*

> *Probably the greatest impact of Project Hope is how it affected my view of mission (p162).*

> *It provided me with a safe setting to explore some questions about ministry that I had not had any other access to prior to coming along to the group (p159).*

> *I come from a very large and very active church. I have (many) opportunities to learn from excellent teaching. But it is often difficult to understand how it works out in the world without the teaching of a group such as Project Hope (p162).*

> *One session that provided a critique on models of church that weren't meeting the needs of a lot of people was helpful. This session gave me much to think about and I was then able to work with my church on developing some*

> *alternative(s) (p160).*
>
> *I now think I can share my faith far more powerfully by really identifying and exploring key "touch-points" in others from which to establish relationships (p164).*

•

While some people were content to simply answer the questions in the survey, other people were prompted to write us letters telling us in greater detail about some of their learnings.

Donna Mulhearn, a peace activist and author of *Ordinary Courage* (Boomerang 2009), wrote:

> *It was at the course that I decided that I wanted to live on the edge, in the chaos, where Jesus is. I now live in community, I am downwardly mobile and live a simple life as a pilgrim. I hope to always live this way because I feel free to serve God in any way I feel led. I have a spirituality rather than a religion, this changes every thing. I am a contemplative, I practice Christian Meditation and this has resulted in greater self awareness. The words of Jesus: "The Kingdom of God is within you" now means something. The course has helped me along my journey of action and contemplation (p127).*

Graeme McKenzie, a teacher at Bowen State Primary School, wrote:

> *In 1995 I stumbled across the Waiters Union. I was excited to experience a group of people putting Christ's teaching into daily practice where the "rubber hit the road." Just as Christ was concerned for the plight of marginalised individuals and groups who were being unfairly*

discriminated against, so too are the Waiters Union.

The Waiters Union interact with social issues in their local area that the vast majority of churches only pay lip-service to. The Micah Challenge is challenging all churches to seek justice for the poor and oppressed. The Waiters Union is fleshing out this plea in their locality and playing their part.

From what I have seen in my 35 years of life, this intentional community of Christ's followers is the closest model of the early church (as expressed in the book of Acts) that I have experienced in Australia.

My exposure to the Waiters Union has been a significant factor in making many changes to my lifestyle:

- *Choosing to live a lot more simply materially.*

- *Cutting back to part-time work in order to be involved in the community.*

- *Utilizing insights from the Waiters Union to help build a sense of "community inclusiveness" within the primary school classroom where I am a teacher.*

- *Joining a "housing working group" within the Baptist Church to seek ways in which the Church could help alleviate the housing crisis that occurs within the community.*

- *Joining a Housing Working Party within Bowen Community, which is investigating strategies that may help alleviate the housing shortages for low income* earners and seasonal workers.

- Building a friendship with a man suffering from schizophrenia and meeting regularly to support and encourage each other.

More recently, my wife and I have chosen to move to Cambodia as a step of faith that Christ demands action if our world is to become "an equal place for all".

(From *Letters In Support Of The Waiters Union* Brisbane 2005 – McKenzie 20/07/05)

Steve Forward, an at-risk youth consultant with Scripture Union (SU) Queensland, wrote:

> My awareness and appreciation of the ministry of the Waiters Union goes back many years. In my early twenties, I found many of the answers to the questions I was asking myself about "real life" faith and ministry in the stories, examples, relationships and opportunities that were provided by the various ministries of the Waiters Union. I would say that some of the key aspects of my current ministry framework came to me through this contact, and I have taken and developed that framework through work as a Social Worker, School Chaplains Trainer of other youth workers and in my Youth a Community role with the church. I believe that the many people I have ministered to and with over the past 15 years have benefited from the influence of the Waiters Union in my life in numerous ways.
>
> Over the years, at least two of the young people from our church moved into West End and became a commit-

ted part of the Waiters Union community for a number of years.

There they lived a model of Christian community and ministry that I believe is not available to be experienced in any other setting in Brisbane, possibly Queensland or Australia. I really appreciate that the Waiters Union was there to open up the possibility of this deep Christian lifestyle experience to these young people of ours. I can see that it has made a significant, deep and lasting impression on them.

I work for SU Queensland and the Waiters Union has played a role in helping SU Queensland through a transition from engaging a narrow range of young people with a short-term specifically-evangelistic focus in artificial settings to engaging with a broader range of young people with a holistic focus in their long term real life settings.

The example of Christian community that is promoted through the Waiters Union and the challenging theological ideas that permeate the movement have been leading lights as we have explored what it means for us to engage hurting communities on behalf of Jesus.

We are currently exploring alternative models of communities of faith in our own community on behalf of our church congregation. The small group of people we have begun this journey with call themselves "the greenspace" and are committed to being a meaningful Christian network that will make more sense to people in our community who have no connection to churches. I find in developing this model, that I am using the examples of the Waiters Union, time and time again, to do those things that (are) the most useful to those outside of established church communties.

(From *Letters In Support Of The Waiters Union* Brisbane 2005 – Foreward 18/07/05)

Geoff Westlake, a co-founder and coordinator of Cheers, wrote:

As a co-founder of Cheers (in Banksia Grove, Western Australia) it's my pleasure to report that the Waiters Union in Brisbane (Queensland) has been the most significant single source of formation for our movement. The example of the Waiters Union, clarified for us our own mission in this neighbourhood, plus gave us ways to begin, and ways to do it effectively and without unnecessary offence.

Cheers has already become an effective holistic Christ-based mission in this community. Recently the residents' association president (not a believer) said, "There's no way Banksia Grove would be the community it is today if it weren't for Cheers." Cheers is yeast in the dough here, growing in favour with the common people, salty.

Not only that, but the Waiters-Union-inspired Cheers story is in turn inspiring other movements here in West ern Australia (on the opposite side of Australia and just about as far away from Brisbane as you can get) through the Forge and Reframe networks. Now we are assisting new plants based on similar grounds as the Waiters Union. Further, we are consulting with existing churches to help them reconfigure their outreaches along similar lines.

From time to time people ask where they can learn more of "this stuff" and I invariably point them to the Waiters Union, and their resources. Besides their great body of input, their continued existence over 25 years shows that such a work is sustainable.

Last week, Forge held its first national summit, and 630 registrants representing hundreds of missions in Australia testify to the current rise of this kind of ministry. National Christian Life Survey is currently researching the "emerging church" phenomenon, recogising its growing role in the future of the Australian church. David Barrett's research in the World Christian Encyclopaedia even suggests that such movements will be the future of the world-wide church, the predominant practice within 20 years.

Clearly the current surge of interest in Cheers and in the Waiters Union is because (its) ministry was before its time, but now that time has come. We are now clearly in a post-Christian time, and a more postmodern culture. A cross-cultural missionary practice is now needed. The Waiters Union offers one of the very few effective, replicable, genuine, missional models of (the future) church in Australia.

(From *Letters In Support Of The Waiters Union* Brisbane 2005 – Westlake 12/07/05)

Dave Andrews and Helen Beazley (editors)

Living And Learning In The Waiters Union
Helen Beazley

My husband and I have thought of ourselves as belonging to the Waiters Union since moving to West End in 2000. We regularly participate in the Monday morning meetings, the weekly community church service, the fortnightly community meal, monthly picnics and six weekly gatherings.

This list of "activities" gives the impression of a program-centric organisation. Of course, the Waiters is anything but.

The "routine" of our involvement with the Waiters reflects our preference for structured interactions. So one of our greatest learnings has been from Waiters who are less activities focused but who constantly open up their lives and homes to people in difficult circumstances and often with difficult behaviours.

As a consequence we have been challenged to relate more freely and flexibly to friends in our community who face various challenges. In fact learning from others' lived convictions, rather than conforming to a prescribed set of rules, seems to be the way of Waiters.

While our household is not vegetarian, the convictions of vegetarians in the group caused us to rethink our eating habits and to be far more concerned with the wellbeing of farm animals. While our household does not home school, the practice of this option by some made us think more deeply about the values we want to impart to our children and the negative cultural influences we want to shield them from.

While our household owns a car, the simple lifestyles pursued by

---

Helen still lives in West End with her husband and two daughters. Her life remains punctuated by the rhythm of Waiters activities.

others in the group has made us determined to minimise our household's private transport requirements.

In other words, my partner and I judge ourselves against the Christ-like practices of others at Waiters, trying to adjust our own values and practices in light of their witness, rather than having "authority figures" or a set of rules sit in judgement over us.

It would be misleading not to allude to some of the frustrations we have experienced. Downplaying structure has sometimes led to things falling into a hole. Sometimes we have felt disappointment at the varying priority given to regular fellowship times. But most of the time we are encouraged by the integrity of people associated with the Waiters network in taking on unpopular causes, befriending unpopular people, and embracing unpopular values like humility, simplicity, and sacrifice.

Who knows what the future holds for Waiters. The gentrification of the area has made it difficult for people wanting to live simply and identify with the poor to make their homes permanently in this locality. The irony was not lost on us when the purchase of our house in West End (for more than we hoped to pay) settled in the same week that a hostel whose residents had long standing relationships with Waiters folk, closed its doors.

Question marks around Waiters' ability to sustain itself and its now iconic programs such as community meal, used to bother me. Now I feel more laid back, a bit more in tune with the original intent of Waiters, which I think is about waiting on those who the mainstream generally passes by, listening, praying, responding, and seeing what happens next.

2005

Learning Theology Through Conversation
Leanne Baker

It's a room which can fit a surprising number of people because, I guess, they're the kind of people who are happy to sit at others' feet before people spill out into the hallway. Basically the only furniture in the room is chairs, lining the walls. There's no hiding that they've all come from various places. And so have the people.

There would be much to disagree on with so many perspectives represented, but the conversation is approached from a different angle; all those perspectives converge on a topic of common interest. The common theme in all these discussions has been about how to most faithfully follow Jesus.

I've been part of theological conversations within the Waiters Union in a group context and with individuals. What's so nurturing about those conversations is that the talk is about "where rubber hits the road," or to put it theologically, How is God, through the person of Jesus Christ, calling us to live?

There is no monotony in this theological chatter; it is animated with the realities and possibilities of how the Spirit is working for the goal of the Kingdom of Heaven being formed on earth. And that's the essential two ingredients of theological conversation: theory and practice.

I understand this "theory" is the grand Story of God, who persistently offers hospitality to people, from the first creative act, to the invitation to covenant, to the Incarnation, to the

---

Leanne has been involved in a faith community with a focus on community development in Brisbane for seven years. She is married to Kenn and they have two boys, Jett and Finn. Leanne completed a Master of Divinity in 2002 and is an ordained minister with the Wesleyan Methodist Church.

sending of the Spirit, and to the anticipation of a feast for the faithful. It's on that Story, surely, that every other story must be understood and they are the stories of us.

Project Hope has been the venue for many theological conversations I've attended. I appreciate the beginning of each one which welcomes each person to give a very brief introduction of him or herself. Some then talk on the topic of the day, and how it intersects with spirituality. Then the space is made for others to talk, and talk we do. I've seen how this space has been safe for vulnerabilities to be disclosed and for questions to be presented. Sometimes we have to be content for the answers to elude us and somehow that's an easier pill to swallow when we're together on the searching.

In 2005–06, I was quite involved in the establishment and running of Crash Beds, a project which offered safe accommodation for homeless, single women four nights each week. The Waiters Union articulated the theological basis for this and it was something that we returned to repeatedly at meetings of the working group. This ongoing theological conversation that wove itself through the pragmatic details of running the project was the lifeblood that sustained all the volunteers' commitment to be inclusive to those so unlike ourselves. Hosting these strangers was a true test of our spirituality and it was a theology of welcome and hospitality that undergirded the experience.

Most recently, during 2009, I was part of some Thursday night discussions which meandered through topics which the group decided. These discussions confirmed the ongoing nature of our conversion, and that discipleship often is the conversion of misguided ways of thinking, being and acting. My sense of these nights is that we weren't shedding spiritual baggage only to pick up a new suitcase, but rather we were discarding that which wasn't helpful and cumbersome to the Spirit so that we could continue on the journey with the essentials. And Lord knows, just the essentials are enough of a challenge.

A particular Thursday night of significance was the inter-faith dialogue with Halim Rane, Deputy Director of the Griffith Islamic Research Unit and Lecturer in the Islamic National Centre of Excellence Studies at Griffith University. We talked that night of violence, of peace, of how far apart we can sometimes stand despite being so close. The ways Halim and his colleagues were working through their faith mirrored, sometimes astoundingly so, the way the Thursday night group had been working through ours.

Then there are the one-on-one spontaneous and chance meetings with people from the Waiters Union. Some, who may have been in our neighbourhood, swung by to catch up, and conversation steered its way to theology, not with heavy words weighted by heavy meanings, but talk of how we're understanding God, God's purposes, the way God operates and wants us to interact. And this often with two toddlers entering the conversation with unrelated simplicities.

There it is, that theology I love: talk of God with friends, this time with those who are in Waiting, in the very ordinary, even mundane, of life and about the ordinary of life. It seems to be a consistent place where God and people interact and grace emerges. And I'm nudged forward that bit more to seek the Kingdom, inhabit it and let it inhabit me.

2010

Learning About Reality Through Immersion
Pete Hawkins

My wife Jenny and I, along with our two boys, Callum and Rowan (then aged five and three) spent two memorable weeks with the Waiters Union in the run up to Christmas 2003.

In truth I approached this trip with no small trepidation. Both Jenny and I were long-term fans of all that the Waiters Union was about, but I felt we were ill equipped. This seemed strange, as with university qualifications in psychology, social work, studies of drug misuse and charity management, I wasn't short of relevant academic knowledge. Having worked for five years as a Probation Officer and the following seven leading a charity that supported Christian drug and homelessness programmes, my professional experience seemed up to scratch too.

But, you see, I was aware that it was one thing to "know" and quite another to experience the realities of total community immersion, 24/7, especially with two young boys. Whilst I'd picked up a good amount of knowledge, this had often been at an arm's length. Moreover I was aware of another downside of this "professional" learning. Although she had walked beside me as I studied and worked, Jenny had not been there in the classroom, the courtroom or the hostel. Her first hand experience was not the same. How would I/she/we cope with the "nowhere to hide" immersion that I expected the fortnight to bring?

We came away not with vastly greater knowledge (though there was certainly some), but with huge growth in our understanding. Our heads hadn't been overly taxed, but our hearts stretched

---

Pete and Jenny live in Somerset, England, with their two sons Callum and Rowan. Pete currently works part time as the UK Operations Director for A Rocha, a Christian environmental mission. Jenny works part time as a tutor for children with special learning needs. In their spare time they are working to restore an organic smallholding.

considerably. We came to a new understanding of an old friend's saying, "some things can only be caught, not taught."

Total immersion was something that I experienced in a number of ways during this fortnight. One of the exercises we were offered was to head out into the neighbourhood and to sleep rough for the night. For my years of involvement with homeless projects and people, this was something I had never experienced. Yet I felt quite safe and smug as I settled for the night amongst the shrubs of a communal garden. However, both feelings were washed away when, at 3.00 am, the night-time watering system started up the sprinklers. No sooner had I worked out that I wasn't the target of a drunkard's urination than my comfy hollow revealed itself to be part of the drainage system! That hadn't happened in the lectures I'd heard about sleeping rough. Spending what remained of the night in sodden clothing was not comfortable, and the feral dogs that arrived before first light to sniff out my subsequent resting place were more than a little threatening. The next-day feelings of exhaustion made me wonder if I should have had greater empathy with those often dirty and grumpy faces that had dragged themselves to the Probation Office two hours late for their 9.00 am appointment.

This time was also an opportunity to discover the underbelly of the Waiters Union. Inevitably the books and papers I had read were written from the author's view point and missed out some detail, especially what was uncomfortable or unresolved. In talking with one Waiters Union "member" I learned how she had given up much to be a part of things, and once a part had continued to give. But over the years her experience of the gap between the publicly espoused ideals and the day-to-day reality had left her with some disappointments and hurts, though she valiantly remained connected, albeit on the periphery. On hearing her story initially I felt disillusioned. Perhaps it was all an unattainable dream, a chasing after rainbows. But through greater reflection and discussion with others, I came to a richer and more profound understanding.

Classroom learning can easily lead to glamorous illusions of the reality and, when everyday life proves rather more complex and messy, the effect can be devastating. I was mindful of fellow journeymen who had "walked away" from similar work; and I was equally cognizant of some of my own disappointment and pain. Yet "held" within the community experience, with the time and opportunity to discuss this reality, I found a deeper harmony with my own life and a greater respect for all that the Waiters Union is about. My own life is "earthed" in the realities of a broken and sinful world and I am a contributor to this damage. As I seek understanding for my own failings, I should extend the same cover to other's shortcomings, though different to my own. Though partial success maybe the best we ever achieve, the perfect can still be held up as a goal – it is a motivating target to aim for. Through the continued commitment of this Waiter, despite the past disappointments, I learned a new approach to some of my own pain; and that we need to hang onto and strive for our dreams even though we know they'll never be achieved. I could have read this in a book, but the impact only came firsthand.

One of our concerns about the community experience was that the intensity would be overwhelming. Again, we learned, through experience, that this can be moderated from the text book ideals. Upon arrival we were offered the use of a house a few streets away (generously entrusted to us by another Waiter away on holiday) with the chance to retire of an evening and ensure the kids got enough sleep. This made the intensity a joy not a burden.

Another unexpected bonus was the sharing of childcare by others on the course. It was a great relief to have others take oversight of our little ones for a while (often to go and buy fresh mangoes). These "sitters" seemed to enjoy the time with our boys too.

One of the profound strengths of the Waiters Union is the hands-on community experience – the community participants, the Waiters community itself as well as the community of the wider district. There is no substitute for actually being a part of things and through the realities, both good and bad, I, and as importantly we, learned together as a family. My past learning and work had not been shared directly by my family. Whilst I could describe my pain when one of the young offenders I was supervising attempted suicide, Jenny didn't know him. These two weeks gave us the chance to narrow that experiential gap.

Yet it extended beyond Jenny and, though young, our boys could also learn. Whilst it was unwise to take our lads rough sleeping on the streets, they could have their own experience. So, a couple of nights after I'd dried out, we slept out in cardboard boxes beneath the house. Callum and Rowan still remember the eerie noises and the challenge of night time toilets six years on, and have an empathy with those for whom this is a regular experience.

One of the deepest and probably the most moving experience was the Christmas party we prepared as a community, for those who would be unlikely to find a welcome elsewhere. The festivity was attended by people with a whole host of personal, social and behavioural challenges. Whilst I'm not sure how well it would have fitted with some of the over-zealous health and safety requirements we experience in the UK (though such a bland and boring, ultra–safe world is not something I want my kids to grow up in) there was enough wisdom and sufficient watching eyes to keep a check on the what and the who.

As someone who is rather jaded by the consumer-driven excesses of our usual Christmas experience, this was a deeply meaningful time. The best china and champagne were substituted for paper plates and lemonade, but it was a time of unbridled celebration; with an honesty and sincerity and an unconditional welcome that more than made up for the lack of fineries. It was also significant for those attending; maybe it was the time of year or the occasion, but a number found a way to talk about their lives as never before. There was fun, there was joking, there was feasting on jam sandwiches and crisps. As guests came to leave, the eye contact made by some who would otherwise never look you in the face spoke of the gift of dignity and human connection they had received.

When our all-too-brief fortnight was over we had learned much that was applicable to coming alongside hurting people. Significantly we had learned as a family, and the strains of such involvement demand the understanding and commitment of the whole. It is not that formalised learning is irrelevant, far from it, but that there were experiential lessons that hadn't been available through our previous endeavour; learning that developed our understanding, perspective and compassion that is all too often lacking in the professionalised world of social care.

2010

Learning To Be Real Through Experimentation
Peter Noble

I work with a guy called Joe. He and I are both lawyers at a Community Legal Centre in Bendigo, Victoria, and we're both Christians.

Together with my wife Delwyn and our three boys I'm part of a couple of alternative Christian experiments – Seeds and The Common Rule.

Joe and I were mutually perplexed one morning when an act of ecumenical decency in Bendigo was crushed by the long arm of Rome. After bits of mortar started to fall off Bendigo's Anglican Cathedral, posing a serious safety risk and forcing a temporary closure, the Diocese was in need of a big church to host some ordinations. The Roman Catholic Bishop made a nearby Catholic Church available for the purpose. At the eleventh hour, once it was discovered that women deacons were to be ordained, the Vatican intervened and forced a venue change!

Joe and I were embarrassed – as Christians. What was the ordinary person to make of this bewildering set of circumstances, rituals and dogma? "People are attracted to the strength of the institution," Joe said, trying to make sense of local fidelity to Rome in the face of the intrusion. "I guess it's what people want."

I immediately recalled rough, whiteboard images contrasting churches as pyramids of power with Christ's scraggly, vulnerable but life-giving vine – drawn during a bible study at the West End Community Orientation Course some 15 years earlier.

Peter was born in Brisbane, the son of a teacher and Anglican minister. He studied Arts Law at The University of Queensland, majoring in Peace and Conflict Studies.
He is Principal Solicitor and Coordinator of the Bendigo based Loddon Campaspe Community Legal Centre. He lives in Bendigo with his wife Delwyn and their three young boys Ciaran, Callum and Daniel.

"Whatever happened to God's Kingdom being like a vine – a fragile but life-giving plant?" I said quietly.

•

I got involved with the Waiters when I was 18 and studying at university. I moved into Highgate Hill with a young couple after we'd done the Community Orientation Course in December 1994. This was the first of five shared houses I was in over about eight years with the Waiters.

I remember one place, on the corner of Middle and Side Streets. Ian Loom and Phil Hall had rented it while I was overseas. When I got back I found that my room was arm's reach away from our neighbour's kitchen and she was fond of late night cook-ups in the pressure cooker. She and her partner got into terrible brawls – she always won. Mike (not his real name) was pretty old and unsteady on his pins. On the first night I was there they had a blue – there was a lot of drinking and yelling. When the pressure cooker started at 3.00 am I wondered, in a sleepy stupor, whether he had finally had enough, done her in and was boiling her down!

We got to know our neighbours well over time – some days were good and some were bad. One day we had to patch Mike up, taking him into his bathroom and dressing some cuts. Many months after they finally separated we noticed that Mike hadn't been having his morning cuppa in the sun. The police told us to have a look in – and we found him dead in his bed.

In some ways our relationships with our neighbours, and each other for that matter, were experiments in love. At their best these experiments were simple, attentive, patient and persistent steps towards community, inspired by the love of Christ. The experiments were inspired, sustained and supported over time through our involvement with the Waiters Union.

The Waiters were tremendously important to me for two reasons. First, they encouraged me to take things personally – not to take responsibility for everything but to be responsive, even if it was in a tiny, seemingly insignificant way. The second was to critically analyse my faith, again through the lens of Christ's love.

Heretics Corner at the Bristol Street household was a ritual weekly gathering of those wanting to talk about things that were, well, heretical! It was very important for me to have open, robust but respectful conversations about my faith. The fact that this could occur within a broader context of care and affirmation by others in the Waiters meant that I could explore my faith amidst people who actually believed God's goodness and grace. It also meant that I could stay grounded – or as grounded as I could given that I am a 5. You know what a 5 is right? (A 5 in the Enneagram is a person who is inclined to be an "observer" not a "doer").

Learning to be grounded was about learning to be real – which I'm still working on! I remember someone once saying, "Jesus calls us to be real, not radical." This was important to me because I felt as though grace and love weren't that important to some radicals. Jim Dowling and Ann Rampa at the Catholic Workers were loving and radical! I first kept bees with Jim Dowling at their place on Mt Mee – I'm still keeping bees at a Biodynamic dairy farm near the Murray River.

Sharing a friendship with Colin Doman, an elderly man (with a love of country music, birds, clocks and dressing up as Santa every Christmas) who lived alone in a Housing Commission flat, helped me to become more real. It helped me understand lots of things better – generosity, loneliness, patience, survival, faith ... .

Going with Aunty Jean Phillips to a maximum security jail to hold a Christmas service with indigenous inmates certainly taught me a bit about reality! Sitting with Eritrean asylum seekers as they prepared coffee the traditional way – freshly roasting beans in small batches – taught me about resilience and hospitality.

I once read a report by Neil Barringham about West End's Community Initiatives Resource Association called *Structuring Without Strangling* (we've set up a similar NGO in Bendigo called Saltbush Community Resource Initiatives!). I think that that title could be applied to the Waiters as well.

There was structure–easily ignored or forgotten or neglected– but structure that supported this fragile experiment in Christian community. Things like the newsletter, Monday morning meeting, gatherings, planning day, mentoring and end of year camp.

Some people need a lot more structure, and I did from time to time. Perhaps more was needed. I feel that an important thing, looking back, was not to expect that the Waiters would be all things – because it could not be. It didn't pretend to be all things – and that was a divine blessing.

2010

A Visitor's View Of The Waiters Union
Nicholas Fiedler

I was about a week away from flying across the world to Australia to spend a year and a half traveling with my wife Leslie. Our goal was to meet new people and create new experiences and I can say with certainty that we accomplished that. While traveling I was also working through my own faith and I asked Brian McLaren to help me out. Brian is a well known author and I explained to him that not only was I going to be out of the country traveling for some time, but also that my faith in God and religion was barely attached to anything real. Brian's suggestion was to make a stop in Brisbane while I was in Australia and to find Dave Andrews. "There is a group he works with down there called the Waiters Union, they're a good group for you."

I had no idea what Brian meant by the phrase, "a good group for you," but when we made it to Brisbane I contacted Dave, who immediately scheduled a time to take my wife Leslie and I out for dinner. We hit it off and started a great friendship. Dave started to introduce me to the people of his locality and I would ask him "Is this what the Waiters Union does?" I would ask him that as homeless people walked up to him and greeted him warmly, as young couples pushed their babies in our direction and they shouted their hellos, I asked him as he showed me his son-in-law and daughter's coffee business, I asked him in the midst of worship gatherings, and dinners.

Even when I had been in Brisbane for two weeks and had interviewed Dave I still couldn't figure out what part of his life was his normal life, and what part of it was the Waiters

---

Nick lives and works in Atlanta, Georgia. He is a writer that works for Apple on the side. He has a wife Leslie, and a dog, McCartney. He recently published his first book, *The Hopeful Skeptic: Revisiting Christianity from the Outside*.

Union. Maybe that is the way it is when you encounter spiritual practices that are shared by a group of interconnected people in a community. The truth is in the month and a half that my wife and I were in Brisbane, I had no idea where Dave's life ended and where the Waiters Union work picked up.

If I were to make a list of all of the activities that I experienced under the umbrella of the Waiters Union I would miss the majority of them and hone in on the smallest of them. Instead I define the Waiters Union through my interactions with Dave.

The first interaction that I had with Dave was when I emailed him and told him that I would be in Brisbane. He emailed back with his phone number. I called him when we arrived in town and he set up a dinner for that night. Dave and Angie picked my wife and I up for dinner and took us to a place across from their house, where they knew the owner – and all of the passersby. My introduction to Dave and the Waiters Union centered around two points: hospitality and community. My wife and I were strangers in Brisbane, but we were welcomed out to dinner and invited to meet the community. Dave didn't just say hello to the passersby, he also introduced Leslie and I to them. The community was contagious and the hospitality never ceased for the month and a half that we were in Brisbane. Dave was constantly calling and inviting Leslie and I to his house, functions he would be at, or gatherings he was involved in. During these gatherings I was meeting more and more of the Waiters, but I wasn't always sure who was a Waiter and who was just out and about and got sucked into a gathering.

One of the big events that I had the privilege to attend a couple times was the fortnightly communal dinner that the Waiters throw for their surrounding community. What I learned about the Waiters through this dinner was that they cared for those that were part of them, but those that seemed to be not like them. The dinners that I attended were attended by a motley crew of Waiters, homeless folks, people living with mental illness, and transient community members. Again Dave picked my wife Leslie and I up in a van and then filled the van with other people that he was collecting from local hostels. Eventually the van filled up and we made our way to the basement of Saint Andrews church. While there the food arrived (both from the Waiters and the guests) and we ate together. As soon as the food line started it was hard to distinguish who was serving and who was the guest. Those that were invited took matters into their own hands by setting up chairs and tables and those that were serving with the Waiters Union blended into the crowd taking their seats next to those they had invited and treating them as guests of honor. When it was time for clean up, everyone helped and the distinction between those who were there to serve and those who were being served disappeared.

The week after the first dinner, I accompanied Dave to the same church basement to be a part of a faith community gathering that consisted of many of the same people that had been at the dinner the previous week. Not only were the disadvantaged present in the community, many were leading the service.

As I have already mentioned, I was only in Brisbane a short time and in addition to the three main events that I described attending, there were apparently many more. But I learned something about the Waiters Union even though most of my understanding about the Waiters Union came from stories of the two main gatherings I had attended. The gatherings weren't the main events of the Waiters Union. They were scheduled events so they were easy to track and talk about, but they weren't the heart of the Waiters Union.

At the heart it seemed that the Waiters were a group of people in the community of West End in Brisbane that had decided to live in covenant. They weren't a church or a faith community. They were people who displayed hospitality in the community. Just like Dave inviting strangers like Leslie and I over to his house, night after night. That was what a Waiter did. Dave introducing Leslie and I to his community and to the events that his community took part in – that was what the Waiters did.

It's true that the Waiters throw dinners for the people that are not like them in their community, but it is more than a dinner every fortnight. The Waiters know their neighbours. They see them on the street, they help them when they can, and they give them more than a dinner a couple times a month. They become part of their lives. They share themselves and they serve. Many at the dinners hug one another. Those that are invited know the children and the lives of some of the Waiters.

This commitment to service and living with "the other" in one's community extends past the divide of the less fortunate. It extends to people of other faiths and nationalities. The Waiters value interfaith conversations not to change the other, but wanting to listen to the other. During my stay I experienced one of the interfaith conversations where I learned what it could look like when people with vast differences spiritually could share themselves wholly without the threat of argument.

It seemed that an open mind was also part and parcel of being a Waiter, which makes sense, because the only way that we can truly be hospitable is if we accept the other without having to change the other. This seemed to be a strong message of all the Waiters I met. Leslie felt this too during our time in Brisbane. She no longer identified with Christianity and was leery about meeting up with a "ministry," but during our time she had nothing but good things to say about each of the Waiters we met. No one assumed she was a Christian, or assumed that she needed to change her beliefs. She had the opportunity to share her stories and her struggles and to serve side by side with people who called themselves Christians and those who didn't.

Invitation, hospitality, community, and acceptance. These were the things I took away from Brisbane. This is what I think the Waiters Union is. It is not an inner-city ministry. It is not a church. It is not even "Christian," but it is "like Jesus". The Waiters serve, they emulate what Jesus sought to teach us about how to treat our neighbour. They are people who bow slightly lower than their neighbours and serve them. The Waiters not only serve their neighbours, but they use the definition of neighbour that Jesus would have used, they use an expanded definition. That definition includes a homeless lady, and it includes an American passing through the city for a few weeks. The Waiters don't take time asking who their neighbour is, they serve whoever is present in their community, anyway they can.

2010

Falling Down The Waiters Union Rabbit Hole
Emily James

Mahatma Gandhi believed that "happiness is when what you think, what you say and what you do are in harmony." I'm inclined to agree with him, and I believe that hanging out with the Waiters Union over the past six months has helped me to bring these three aspects of my life closer together.

My involvement with the Waiters has created spaces to "walk the talk" – living out what I have been writing and thinking about whilst studying community development. In particular, these spaces have helped me to work through my religious prejudices to engage in dialogue with "the other," express my spirituality communally as well as individually, and to feel connected to more of the many worlds that exist in my West End neighbourhood.

Whilst I had heard whispers about the Waiters Union (including the prerequisite confusion – you're part of a union for West End waiters?!) it wasn't until I went to a community development conference that I met my first bona-fide Christi-anarchist. I was feeling a little disillusioned with the workshops I was attending – I was looking for less professionalism and more heart.

So I found myself at the "Community Development and Spirituality" workshop, and was part of a circle of community development workers sharing the motivations behind their vocations. It was a rare privilege to be in a roomful of people attempting to articulate their spirituality and how it linked to their everyday worlds – and I wanted more of it.

Two conversations and two days later I walked half a block

Em lives a stone's throw away from 69 Thomas St. Em likes the blender-sharing Waiters neighbours, circus tricks and talking in Swedish. Em doesn't like gendered language and is very happy to have escaped university for a semester or two. Right now Em is working at a community centre, playing soccer in frocks (aka "froccer") and practising theatre for change – whilst plotting the next adventure.

from my home to arrive at 69 Thomas St and start an intensive Community Orientation Course with people who turned out to be my neighbours. I was understandably wary, having no idea of what to expect (a cult? religious fanatics? were they going to try to convert me?!) and knowingly engaging with Christianity for the first time since high school.

Yet, as I discovered over the next two weeks, the Waiters Union espouses a radical re-interpretation of the "Christianity" I was taught and rejected as a teenager. It was intriguing to meet people with startlingly similar critiques of religion to my own – yet who have chosen to seek out the truth in their tradition, rather than throw the baby out with the bath water.

The challenge, then, was to face up to my own prejudices and look beyond the religious discourse (which was confronting) and instead to seek the essence of what people were saying (which often resonated beautifully).

Building a relationship with members of the Waiters Union has required everyone involved to practise the very principles of dialogue that all of our traditions advocate. In seeking to understand rather than debate, to refrain from judgement and instead remain open to each other's truth, we have been able to translate each others words and recognise ourselves in them.

For example, I greatly respect the Waiters Union for intentionally creating communal spaces to acknowledge our struggles as humans in a hard and beautiful world. Part of this commitment is a time of "open prayer" during community fellowship, where people share their lives with each other and their God. The honest sharing of this fellowship is the only "religious" gathering that has ever moved me. Though the discourse isn't my own, I still feel like the space is open enough for me to participate – I just say "World, hear our prayer" where others say "Lord, hear our prayer."

Such experiences provided me with a practical exercise in how we can break down the comfort zones we create for ourselves – to challenge our tendency to surround ourselves with people who think and experience the world similarly. Through the Waiters Union I have been able to experience more of the many worlds that exist in my street and suburb.

Before finding out about the Community Orientation Course, I had planned on travelling to Melbourne – in the end I felt I had been travelling anyway, moving through the different realities in my neighbourhood. I remember how overwhelmed I felt the first time I went to Community Meal, where people from all walks of life are equally welcome to share dinner and conversation. I recognized numerous people whom I had seen on the streets in West End, yet for the first time had a context within which to introduce myself and share stories.

Months later, I am able to chat when I run into those same people outside the mobile food van, or on the bus. I feel relatively comfortable in conversations with people whose framework is Christianity, wave to everyone sitting in the garden outside 69 Thomas St, and share daily life and food processors with my neighbours.

One quote from the course that has resonated with me is the idea that, "violence is when we forget we belong to each other" – I am grateful for those moments where we can remember we belong to each other. This belonging is quite obvious if you fall down the Waiters Union rabbit hole. The Waiters network has quiet links to many aspects of my suburb that I hadn't previously realised were connected (hence my joking term, the West End mafia).

Turns out that my friends' grassroots groups utilise the space at 69 Thomas Street which is also base for the Waiters Union, my lecturers are part of a related Community Development Co-op that some Waiters Union people helped start, and best of all, I found the perfect location to write my essays for uni – Blackstar (a local fair trade coffee shop run by a couple of people who are part of the Waiters Union). Conversations with other coffee drinkers have proven to be the perfect amount of stimulation (aka distraction).

To me these regular and informal interactions reflect my favourite definition of community as the "creation of space for people to come together" whilst encouraging the "co-existence of difference" (Arai and Pedlar 2003).

For me, this greater awareness of the many connecting threads of people working for change generates the courage to continue, rather than feeling overwhelmed within my individual bubble.

As Ani DiFranco sings, "I know there is strength in the differences between us and I know there is comfort where we overlap". We might have travelled here by different means, but we are here – and we can work together in our communities for similar ends.

2010

Air, Water, Earth, Fire And The Waiters Union
Marty Richards

For many of us who have sought to explore alternatives to mainstream church culture and church culture lifestyles, the Waiters Union has been like a fifth element (i.e. air, water, earth, fire ... and the Waiters Union).

The analogy of the elements is apt as a framework for appreciating the Waiters Union.

Air – the first element–represents the fact that for me (and I would say others also) we needed some space to re-oxygenate as it were, to catch our breath after years of giving institutional church a crack and feeling somewhat worn out and "out of breath" from the struggle.

So the Waiters Union, in the form of relationships and opportunities to give and receive and simply share life/faith together, offered the breathing room necessary to look at redefining what a Christian spiritual journey means outside of the four walls of the institutional church.

Realising that it is actually possible to breathe outside of the structured church was a pleasant surprise. When I first arrived in West End I already had a strong feeling that one could survive as a Christian outside of steeple houses but it was nonetheless quite a big relief that I could keep a simple, active faith going outside the traditional church format (even though I realised quickly that it was in many ways much harder than I expected).

Marty was brought up in Melbourne where he studied music and community development. He moved to Brisbane and married Evonne with whom he has two children, Lila and Kaedin. He is interested in alternative sustainable economics and has started two social ventures – Ethical Property Management (EPM) and Blackstar.

In fact I would say that being a Christian outside traditional church means that you're in a space whereby you almost have to create church as you go, almost at times it seems, on your own. However, knowing that others in the network are feeling the same way is a great support. (But I am digressing from the analogy of elements.)

The second element –Water – would represent the hospitality aspect of the Waiters culture. It was – and, in many ways, still is – refreshing for me to be here amongst so many others who are working through faith issues outside of mainstream expressions of Christian lifestyle.

From early on in my time here (I completed the Community Orientation Course in 1992 and moved to West End in 1995) hospitality was always a core value of many associated with the network. Providing an open door to many locals for whom closed doors had been a significant recurrent experience – and serving loads of refreshing cold water, especially in the Brisbane summer, has been at an essential part of that experience.

The third element is Earth. When I first arrived at the Waiters Course (with Neil and Penny Barringham, Jason McCleod and others) I was given a folder holding the course outline and handouts, and there atop our folder of readings, was a map of West End.

I've always believed that the Waiters Union is what it is because of two main factors – people and place. There is no doubt the Waiters network has brought together a bunch of talented and faithful people, who have (mostly) all chosen to live in or around a very unique place called West End. However, without the earth we call West End (Indigenous name "Kurilpa") I am not convinced the Waiters would exist as it does, purely because Kurilpa is such a "one off" phenomenon of a place both in terms of culture, geography and history.

Last year we were welcomed onto the land for the first time. A local Indigenous Elder (Aunty Mulinjali) ran the ceremony and one of the things I remember her saying is that the land remembers. Given that Kurilpa has been a meeting place for Indigenous communities for a very long time, perhaps some of the land's memory has rubbed off on the Waiters Union.

While we're on the topic of earth, for those who remember our good friend Dr Rodney Farley who used to visit us every day at Bristol St community house throughout the 90s – who could forget Dr Rod's map drawings that he came up with each week entitled "A new map of West End" (I must be entitled to at least one random story about "the good ole days").

Now onto the fourth element – Fire. This is where the analogy could start to tire – as all of the most memorable analogies may – where you want to over contort what you're wanting to say, so it fits the metaphor. But no, seriously, there is a place for Fire in the story. I think it has to do with critical reflection and the role of "controlled burning" of old lifestyle choices.

Looking at my life, I ask myself how am I living out my faith in practical terms? How does my wealth here in Oz affect others who are less well off over there in the rest of the world? Am I part of the problem or am I part of the solution? It's kind of a binary way of approaching things. But fire is fire after all. In a way we are confronting ourselves with all or nothing decisions we need to make if we are wanting to take the Christian spiritual journey seriously. And it comes at the cost of comfort. For many of those that I have shared with throughout my time with the Waiters, this kind of struggling and burning has been a big part of community life.

Fire is also related to "passion" and to the "prophetic" and I would definitely say that the Waiters network has had more than its fair share of prophets and prophetesses over the years. What I love about the Waiters is that despite all the prophets and prophetesses that have come through the network very few have prophesied fire and brimstone onto others in the network who have disagreed with them or approached things differently. There remains a deep respect for one another's journeys different though they may be.

The fifth element is the Waiters Union itself. For me personally the network (in real terms the significant relationships that comprise the network and the committed people who have continued to keep the network meetings going when many – myself included – have ebbed and flowed along the edges) represents a clear sense of place, identity and support. It has informed and is interwoven in the history and context of my present life with Evonne and others in our community economic development work. Without the ongoing connection to the Waiters I would definitely say we wouldn't have progressed community enterprise to the extent that we have to date.

Arriving at Blackstar Headquarters I am always amazed that I keep returning to Thomas St, just a few doors down from the House of Freedom where I first arrived at the Waiters course.

2010

Songs, Guitars, Rockstars And The Waiters Union
Peter Branjerdporn

I have always been involved with music. My parents played in a band together. I sang in a boys' choir for six years, won a few talent quests in high school, and have always played guitar and sung at church. By 18 I was ready to rock the world. With original songs dating back to when I was 12, I was looking for a group of people who would take my music and spread it to the masses. I dreamed of having thousands, no, millions of people singing my songs, and feeling what I feel, appreciating the insights and expression of love and intense emotions from deep within me. After a couple of years of trying, I knew it was not gonna be an easy road, and that a loyal group of friends who not only like your music, but appreciate you for who you really are, is not that easy to come by.

Well, I have felt like a rockstar in my network of friends in West End over the past few years. It's hard to explain, because it's not the rockstar-dom that most wannabe's would have chosen. It's probably more (Monty Python's) The Life of Brian than Jesus Christ Superstar. Let me try ... .

Today, for example, I just got off the train at Central when my friend Dave greeted me in the tunnel. He's a Big Issue vendor in the city, and West End local who hangs out with us. He loves my music. We always talk about who's playing in town and how expensive the tickets are. He lets me know how much he enjoys it when I play guitar at church. Quite a few people do. And they really mean it. You can tell because they sing really loudly. Playing and singing with these guys is always fun and unpredict-

---

Raised in Bangkok, pharmacist and musician Peter B tries to live intentionally with his partner, baby and five friends near West End.

able. We regularly sing unusual songs like What A Wonderful World, Lean On Me, Shackles (by R&B group, Mary Mary), and I Still Cry Daily To Jesus (Casey Chambers). Something amazing happens when you sing "non–church" songs in church. For me, it's like somehow God is present in all of life. We can hear God through pop radio because he created everything, and even in its most corrupted form music has the potential to bless us. We also sing quite a few songs written locally.

Many of the songs are written by another friend, Dave Andrews. He asked me to help him record a handful of his originals a few years back. We had a great time recording live in a church basement, in Paulie B's Tanuki Lounge in West End, and with Andrew Kennedy at his home studio, working with a range of talented musicians who understand the value of community, and the importance of music as one of our most important catalysts. I love the gritty-ness of these "valley songs" (not Hillsongs!), songs that speak to our hearts in the dark moments. Songs that don't ignore reality. Songs that acknowledge the pain, struggle, injustice and disillusionment of life, and stay in the shadows just long enough for you to get a glimpse of what true transformation might feel like. Songs you're not embarrassed to sing in public. I've even performed some in venues around town.

One of the venues in West End is Blackstar. This little espresso bar and its early struggles with Council has been an inspiration to a few of us locals. Marty and Vonney have opened it up for local artists to express themselves through music, poetry, and even the humble chalk-art. Since January 2009 we've had all kinds of performances from local singer-songwriters through to touring international artists, hip-hop to avant-garde folk, slam poetry to blues and roots, electro-glitch to funky jazz. I love the fact that you can walk past Thomas Street on a Saturday night and never quite know what you'll hear. There's something real and organic about the place, the music, the coffee and the people. Even when you don't dig the music, you can still feel the love. A lot of my friends who play there keep telling me how much they enjoy the ambience and the respectful audience.

Words Or Whatever, a monthly poetry showcase at the cafe has been one of the biggest blessings in our lives over the past year. I've really enjoyed witnessing these post-modern lamentations and psalms, subversive verses, and simple expressions of the people, a true open-mic in our censorship-obsessed times. From humble beginnings to getting asked to perform as a collective at Greenfest, our friends help us believe that there is something here worth sharing. We even closed the street with the help from Brisbane Festival in October 09 to celebrate what West End is all about: the people, the old but charming shopfronts, the diverse culture, and the music. The Street Party proved that you don't need to fly in some big-name artist to get people out to a festival ... if you have real friends!

I've met some of my really good friends through the arts. Greg played keyboard with me at a TEAR dinner, took me to help lead music at a MICAH Network gathering in Thailand a year later, then filled in for our band at the street party. Luka (Lesson MC) turned up at our place one day to freestyle on a song I wrote about Blackstar and a year later we were like brothers. Thomas (Dissent Of Didymus) blew me away with his spiritual-socio-political spoken word at the Lex Wotton Fundraiser and, especially now that we live in the same household with our partners, continues to inspire me to be more compassionate, subversive, spiritual and creative with my art and also my life. Another new friend, Aaron has done a few local workshops with me around spirituality and the arts, got a few of us to star in his ambitious Earth Anthem music video project, and runs a fortnightly "doco & soup night" at our place.

I think I've learned a big lesson over the past few years. There was a time when I wanted to rock the world so badly that when I said, "it's all about the music," what I really meant was "it's all about MY music." Nowadays I think I play and sing for the joy of connecting with people, chilling with friends and creating community.

Don't get me wrong, I still like to be praised and adored, of course! I still need to wake up to myself everytime I get into rockstar mode, but at least I'm starting to feel that there are deeper reasons to sing and create and share with each other, through pleasure and pain.

This might sound like a big call, but you know that feeling, and healing, you get when you're at a festival with thousands of people all singing the same song written by some famous rockstar? I feel like that everytime we sing together at our gathering on Sunday nights. I think that's why some people are chronic-festival-goers. Because they don't have friends like mine.

2010

Hippies, Ideals, Realities And The Waiters Union
Christel Palmer

Many years ago when I was a school chaplain I read *The Irresistible Revolution* by Shane Claibourne who is from a community in Philadelphia called The Simple Way. What Shane talked about in this book seemed to me to be the answer to a lot of questions I had about the institutionalized church and its inability to connect with the suffering in the local community – the needs I saw working with at-risk youth in the local high school.

I had heard of the Waiters Union through various training sessions Dave had done with Scripture Union even back in 2000 and the idea of the Waiters Union had always appealed to me. For many years I mulled over what was talked about and sat on the fringes of the 6.30 pm service at St Andrews. But it wasn't until I had decided to leave chaplaincy and move back home to save to go to India that I had the time and the space to consider moving into West End and living in an "intentional community household."

Going to India for me was a big shake up. I saw first hand the effects that my lifestyle had on the poor and how the injustice of the way I lived impacted on the lives of so many. I knew that when I got back to Australia I could not go on living the same middle class lifestyle I had been living. Things had to change, but I couldn't do it on my own, I needed other like minded people around me to help me make the changes I needed to make.

Christel grew up in a Christian family in Redcliffe, north of Brisbane. She studied at the Catholic University and did youth ministry and school chaplaincy. She has joined the Waiters Union, where she is exploring intentional community, and Scripture Union, where she is training young people in youth work.

So when I returned to Australia in March 2008 I moved into West End and helped set up the Princhester Street House, an experiment in living in community and engaging the wider community with other young adults. It has been quite a journey and I've learnt a lot about community and myself.

My major learning has been that *you can't force people to live up to your ideals (especially ones you can't live up to yourself) and you need to be patient on the journey, learn together and strive together to do the most difficult thing – really love – in a less than ideal world.*

When I first moved to West End it was important for me to learn that the Waiters Union is not a community but a network. Some people are tightly knitted to each other in community – either by vocation, location or friendship – and others are loosely woven together by association or similar values. I had to put energy into building connections with people, initiating friendships, joining with others in different activities or getting things happening.

Community did not happen automatically, but I had access to people who were more open than my experience of the average bunch of people in the suburbs I'd lived in.

The Waiters Union has been a great context for me to make this and many other discoveries. My connection with the network has given me access to many quality people with lots of experience in community and particular issues that I was interested in. I have had a space in which I can deconstruct and reconstruct my theology and work out what it means for us to follow Jesus in our society in today's world.

I have had the opportunity to explore several lifestyle issues. I have had the opportunity to particularly explore the way I relate to Aboriginal people and people with disabilities. I have challenged myself not to get paid to love and serve people, but to do it out of my compassion for "the marginalised" and my desire to be a good neighbour. Inviting people – whom I would not have otherwise connected with – into my home has been one of the most special things that has come from my connection with the Waiters Union. I still have a long way to grow in making space for these people in my life, but my experience so far has definitely touched my heart.

More than the structured ways of learning such as the Community Orientation Course and the many other groups within the Waiters Union, it has been the people I have met and the way they live their lives that has influenced me most. I have also been exposed to alternative ways of engaging the world that are more simple, more sustainable, more peaceful and more non-violent. I have also been exposed to practical ways I can make a statement about the wastefulness of the system we live in by learning to dumpster dive.

Many people come to stay at our place on Princhester Street to check out the Waiters Union. I often say to them, "You may not see much happening this week. We're just normal people with normal lives trying to experiment with some different things ... it's a bit of a *choose your own adventure sort of thing*."

For many years on what I could call "my journey out of the institutional church and into community" I articulated my frustration in a way that was not matched by the way I lived. I stuck around with the institutional church for a long time trying to change them and the way they worked and finally realized that I needed to get out there and change myself and the way I lived. "Actions speak louder than words," as they say.

I have found that being involved with the Waiters Union has provided a safe space to travel from the beliefs based religion of the institutional church to the radical action based faith that Jesus really calls us to. I still have a long, long way to go in really living out the gospel and dealing with my addiction to the dominant values of society, but I feel that I've also come a long way from where I was.

To be honest it was easy for me to swing from being a fundamentalist "right-wing conservative Christian" to being a fundamentalist "left-wing hippy Christian" (as some people call us) and I have very much been in that space, judging other Christians harshly. I guess that is pretty normal when you have reacted against something that disappointed you so deeply.

But I am learning not to throw the baby out with the bathwater, to find some value in where I have come from and to rediscover a more contemplative, less judgmental, Jesus-based spirituality that is more consistent with my new (and continually developing and constantly changing) understanding of who God is and his/her vision for our world.

In some ways it would have been easy for me to give up on institutionalized Christianity altogether (and I think I did for a while); but for now I have gone back to working for the conservative Christian organization I previously worked for when I was a chaplain. I have found that, with the help of some friends there, I can actually work constructively towards more inclusivity, diversity, community, peace and justice.

2010

Love, Adventure, Nonviolence And The Waiters Union
Jason MacLeod

I wasn't the standard Waiters Union recruit, if such a person exists.

When I arrived to attend the Orientation Course in December 1992 I was the only non-Christian enrolled. More unusual still for a course that was explicitly orientated towards Christ's way of building community in a troubled world, I was anti-Christian! Jesus as a person was alright I reasoned; it was the Christians who really bugged me. At the time I had just returned from Papua New Guinea, West Papua, and Indonesia disgusted by what had been done in the name of Christianity. What seared my soul was not the sharing of the gospel of love and solidarity, which did occur in places, but the destruction of local culture, the appropriation of Indigenous land, and in the case of West Papua, Christian missionary support of military occupation. It took me some time to make the connection that Jesus, Christians and Christianity were not necessarily the same thing, and that faith can be a resource for transformation. It was with and through the Waiters that I made that journey.

But back then I had another problem. I may not have liked what some Christians were on about, but I was impressed by what some of them were doing. In fact, when I looked around it was often the Christians who were doing what I felt needed to be done: not only care for the oppressed but also nonviolently work to change the systemic causes of their oppression. More

---

Jason lives in a co-housing set-up in Inala, Brisbane with his partner Manon, their two kids, another family, and aspirations to raise chickens. He works as a social worker, accompanying refugees and coordinates a nonviolence education and training project in the Asia-Pacific region. Whenever possible he likes to have a long walk in the bush.

than anything I was looking for people who were really committed to changing the world.

When I first left school – and I blush at the naivety of this now – I thought that the best way to serve others was to be a professional helper. So I enrolled in social work at university. Later, I realised what the world really needed was not so much dispassionate professionals administering the welfare system, but people prepared to give something of themselves, in a sustainable but committed way, for the good of everyone.

So after returning from travelling I began to look for folks who wanted to change the world, not only as social workers or activists, but also as ordinary people, as friends willing to get alongside those living on the margins of society. My problem was that I found it was the folks at the Waiters Union and the nearby Catholic Worker house who were really "walking the talk." That is why I cautiously decided to do the Orientation Course and that is how I ended up with the Waiters.

Three key themes stand out for me as I reflect back on my time with the Waiters Union: a commitment to specific people and being grounded in a particular place, crossing boundaries, and experiments with nonviolent action.

People and place

For most of my life I had moved around. This was partly fuelled by adventure, but it also masked a flight from intimacy. As long as I kept moving I would not have to face my inner demons, the incidents and patterns in my life that caused pain to me and others. This might have been ok except for the fact that without being prepared to deal with hurt caused and experienced in our life, transformation would be impossible. So one of the first steps in my healing was making the decision to stay put; committing to a specific place and the people who lived there.

Bristol Street – a supportive household for people who wanted to build local community and deepen their faith – provided the vehicle for me to do this. Of course I didn't recognise this at the time. Initially I was looking for a place to do my third year social work placement. I sure as hell wasn't looking to deepen my faith, I was after a "boots and all" experience of community work. I would just have to tolerate the "Christian bit," I reasoned. I said I would give living in Bristol St six months. I stayed for two and a half years. In terms of committing to people and place I could talk a lot about the folks who stayed and visited, many of them folks marginalised by a society geared towards consumption and production, but just as significant for me was the experience of living with other Bristol Street residents.

I recall one weekly house meeting in particular. Summer holidays were fast approaching and I had planned another adventure, mountaineering and bushwalking for six weeks with friends in Aotearoa (New Zealand). Of course I wanted to do the right thing and let people know when I would be leaving, so I announced my decision at the house meeting. Imagine my shock when people started discussing whether I could go or not! Let's leave aside the fact that I had already paid for my ticket, this was my life! What the hell were people doing trying to tell me what to do!

Margaret (not her real name), one of the long-term Bristol St residents at the time – a woman who taught herself to read and write at Bristol St and then went on to teach folks with learning disabilities and mental illness living in the psychiatric hostels around West End to do the same – tried to explain it to me.

"Jason," she said, "what we are trying to do here is build community together; how can we do that if you aren't here; if you keep coming and going at a moment's notice?"

Margaret challenged me to commit to community. Relationships are at the heart of building community. A changed world is made up of transformed relationships. Without hanging around, day in day out, through the tough times as well as the good times, it is impossible to build relationships. That was when I started to see my wanderlust in a new light. Slowly, and not without difficulty, committing to specific people in a specific place started to become a new type of adventure for me, a spiritual, emotional, mental and personal challenge to complement more physical ones.

Crossing boundaries

Once I began to frame building community as an adventure, all sorts of opportunities opened up. I threw myself into the work of refugee resettlement. Here was a chance to travel the world without even leaving my neighbourhood! Accompanying individuals and families from El Salvador, Guatemala, East Timor, Vietnam, Eritrea, and Iraq was incredibly challenging and enriching. I also confronted a reality that our society was not the welcoming hospitable place that I longed it to be.

There is a theory in popular education that there are three zones of learning: the comfort zone, the discomfort zone, and the alarm zone. The thinking is that we learn most when we move out of our "comfort zone" and into the "discomfort zone" but are not pushed so far that we enter the "alarm zone" and shut down. The role of an educator or facilitator is to help create the context – the trust and safety – and experience for people to leave their comfort zone and enter the "discomfort zone" where rich learning, and sometimes even transformation, can take place. Entering the discomfort zone where we are open and receptive to learning has been so helpful to me, that I now welcome the feeling of discomfort because I know I will learn and grow. Accompanying refugees was an experience of learning through getting out of my comfort zone. Of course for many people who have arrived in Australia as refugees, trying to build a new life in Australia is nearly always profoundly uncomfortable and disorientating.

For me, crossing boundaries was not about abandoning a separate sense of self, or about relating to others in ways that were less than healthy, it was essentially about being willing to let go of what I was sure of. Getting uncomfortable for me was about learning words and phrases from other languages, being willing to sit in the discomfort of a three day wake, not having a clue what was going on around me, developing cross-cultural friendships, and learning about how to negotiate with mainstream society from the perspective of the refugee experience.

In time relationships blossomed into experiments: a multi-faith support group, endless picnics, camps, and other things. Together with three friends we even formed a multi-lingual, multi-cultural women's worker cooperative where I was the "honorary woman" and all of us had to use a second language at least some of the time, because none of us had a common language. In many respects it was a disaster: people got food poisoning, we barely made a cent, and one time when we ran what we called the "rainbow café," a food and film night, we showed a film we hadn't previewed which turned out to be soft Latin porn! But the co-op went for over six months. The women learnt a bit more English, two of the three got employment, the third started full-time English classes, and we were all enriched in some way. Crossing boundaries became a commitment to welcome and learn from the stranger.

Experiments with nonviolent action

While accompanying refugees allowed me to respond to those who were the victims of war, experimenting with nonviolent action against militarism enabled me to address some of the causes of war. Inspired by other folks in the Waiters Union, including Catholic Workers, some of us formed a small group working for a free East Timor. Together we engaged in creative nonviolent action. We met with officers of the Australian Army to explain our willingness to try and interrupt their support for organised violence in East Timor. They of course told us they were only following orders.

One time a group of us walked from Brisbane to the Canungra Land Warfare Centre, an Australian military base specialising in counter-insurgency operations. It was here, in the Gold Coast hinterland that the Australian government trained members of the Indonesian military, including Kopassus, the notorious Special Forces who were forming militia groups and committing human rights violations in what was then occupied East Timor. When we arrived at the Land Warfare Centre we nonviolently entered the base to establish an office for conscientious objection. Our goal was to encourage members of the Australian military to follow their conscience before orders.

We were of course, arrested, taken to court, and after refusing to pay our fines we went to gaol. We had fund raised the amount of the fine and instead of paying it to the state we sent it as a donation to support community development projects in East Timor. Experimenting with nonviolent action was profoundly liberating. Above all I learnt to deal with my fear. Going to gaol deepened my solidarity with East Timorese, West Papuans and others incarcerated for resisting oppression. It also deepened my commitment to further experiment with nonviolent action. In all of this my main guide was Gandhi, a Hindu, a bloke who I reckon was the greatest Christian of the 20th century. Gandhi called his exploration of nonviolence experiments with Truth. For Gandhi this was all about living out his values and beliefs in light of trying to transform himself, build a network of inter-related self-managed communities, and nonviolently confront the roots of injustice. This was Gandhi's path towards knowing the nonviolent God of peace, love and justice.

I wasn't always aware of it at the time but committing to specific people living in a specific place, accompanying and learning from those on the margins, and experimenting with nonviolent action, led me towards God. Folks in the Waiters Union didn't try and shove Jesus down my throat, they simply created space for me to discover the spirit for myself and commit to the work of building a better world in practical ways. I don't always call myself a Christian because I am not sure I always share the same understanding of what that means with others. I don't think it matters. Clinging to labels, identity and lifeless rote invocations seems a little like voodoo to me. But I long to be drawn towards Christ. The practices I learnt at the Waiters Union still draw me down that path.

2010

Ways We Have Learnt To Walk With Indigenous Australians
Neil Hockey

After years of engagement with Aboriginal people, Aunty Jean, a local Aboriginal leader, asked us to run an Indigenous Community Orientation Course. The course would help non-Indigenous people begin the long-term processes of building healthy and informed relationships with Indigenous people; learning more about Aboriginal historical experiences, their strengths and struggles; and thinking how to go about building authentic partnerships with personal integrity and for social justice through community development, at the initiative of local families.

Overall, we facilitated an intensive (both inner and outer) immersion experience in an Aboriginal community development context, managing the process between four facilitators. The course was run in the Beaudesert-Logan area south of Brisbane.

Most full-time (and some part-time) participants were prepared through an initial expression of interest process, informal face-to-face or phone interviews and the provision of some minimal carefully chosen pre-reading.

Aboriginal leaders were engaged to conduct structured sessions and forums. We also provided a balance to these sessions by enabling other learning experiences emerging from activities and relationships in the local communities.

We worked sensitively with participants to process their experiences one-to-one, in small groups and as a whole group.

Neil was born in Brisbane and is currently employed at the Centre for Poverty and Development Studies, Kuala Lumpur, involved in participatory action research with Indigenous groups and others across Australasia. Together with Lim Siew Chin, Neil has two children, one working in South India and the other in Melbourne.

We began with a process of introductions, sharing hopes, concerns and expectations in order to develop a Working Agreement that would form the basis for ongoing group and debriefing processes.

We maintained a daily and overall program rhythm where cycles begin and conclude with allowing space and time for participants to listen deeply to God, themselves and each other.

We covered topics such as:

- theological and cultural bases of values, worldviews and frameworks for justice
- traditional art and craft, bush tucker and medicine
- local history and land significance
- contemporary social, economic and political realities
- potential for ongoing relationships and partnerships, and
- community development in Aboriginal contexts.

Twenty people (including four facilitators and one child) participated in the course full time (8–10 days) including camping overnight, with about 40 more part timers or people who joined in a session or meal. These figures far exceeded our expectations.

Almost half of these participants were of Aboriginal and/or Islander descent. From written and verbal feedback participants sensed with excitement, the potential for building much further on relationships within and between the cultural groups represented.

A major result was the commitments made to begin processes of building authentic partnerships with integrity, with Aboriginal and/or Torres Strait Islander people in at least nine specific places in southeast Queensland: Gold Coast, Beaudesert, Logan,

Inala, Ipswich, Inner city Brisbane, Wynnum, Bracken Ridge and Narangba. We acknowledge that there needs to be a lot of prayer and careful thought yet, so as to plan strategically while anticipating surprises in seeing what God might do as we pray, plan and act.

Community participation

In Beaudesert the Mununjali Housing and Development Company made available their 2.5 acre site with hall and facilities. They also enabled access to vehicles for transport to the overnight bush-camp. Four local families loaned equipment for use and members from three of those families participated in the course. In Logan the response was even more widespread, with some community participants joining in from Northern New South Wales church groups.

Community capacity building

The project arose from long-term relationships (including cross-cultural) both within and between local communities. By linking with existing local knowledge and initiatives, the project has served as an extra catalyst. The ongoing vision is broadening and deepening, strengthening capacity not just in Logan and Beaudesert, but right across a region stretching from Cherbourg through the greater Brisbane area down to Fingal and Lismore in New South Wales.

Engagement after the course

After the course, participants linked into events put on by Indigenous organisations, contributed to Invasion Day prayer and ensuing activities, initiated a Make Indigenous Poverty History group in Brisbane and are contributing to similar prayer and other action groups across the region.

As a direct follow-up from the course, 14 people completed a two-day campout over Easter, back at the bush-camp site in Beaudesert region. With all of these strategies, fortnightly or monthly events were planned to continue and broaden, while linking with each other in a strategic manner.

Constraints encountered

The main problems that arose during the course were that of tiredness, less than optimal reflection time, and the issues surrounding photos being taken. Towards the end of the course at Logan some of the activities were made optional to ensure that those who were running out of energy could have some time to themselves.

The issue of protocols around photography was a difficult one. Some felt that the frequency and manner of photo-taking was too intrusive at times. The matter was addressed on a one-to-one basis earlier. It was then discussed in a group forum. However, this was probably a bit late in the course. The issues surrounding the taking of photos will clearly need to be covered more directly in the Working Agreement at the start of the course in future. This is especially so because of the sensitivities around recording of any kind in Indigenous communities.

Otherwise there were few problems. Participants worked in the large group and small groups to reflect on the progression of the course and their own wellbeing and personal reactions.

The participants' reports were positive about the shared duties, the facilities and the group times. A few participants in their feedback asked for more small group time to ensure that the airspace is shared in a safer and more even way.

Encouragements experienced

The times with Uncle John Long and Aunty Ruth and their families was very much appreciated and enjoyed in Beaudesert, especially the overnight trip to their traditional country ("the Hollow"). The evenings in Logan were noted as a highlight for many people. The focus of music in the evenings gave a great starting place for connections to be made and conversations to begin. However, for some there was a concern that the relationships that had been formed were not of the lasting kind. Participants enjoyed the bush tucker session with Uncle Joe Kirk.

The dinner at Ewing Park was another event that formed a forum for positive interaction between the group and the local people. The opportunity to unobtrusively join in meals, music and games during these times at Ewing Park, the Beaudesert Park and the evenings in Logan were very special. One of the greatest outcomes from the community viewpoint was their enthusiasm over being able to get together as families, in a context where they could learn more about their own histories and cultures, while doing this in a wider group where they were acknowledged and appreciated.

These activities provided time for not just fun but active experiential knowledge. They engaged the course participants with the local elders who shared their knowledge and experiences of being Indigenous in Australia with great courage and humility. These times were exciting in the sense of anticipation of things to come. Being able to be actively involved in activities and places as well as sessions of listening and questioning provided a greater level of knowledge and understanding of the struggle of Australia's Indigenous peoples.

Some participant reflections:

> *Often in the past when I've thought about becoming involved with Indigenous issues I've felt overwhelmed and isolated. This course helped build some genuine relationships and gave me confidence that there is a place for my involvement in seeing better outcomes for Indigenous people. My husband and I want to journey alongside Aboriginals but have often had no idea where to begin with our passion. This course gave us a lot of hope and a beginning for how and where we can connect with Aboriginals. We both felt our passion and determination to be involved increase throughout the duration of this course.* Rebecca

> *The course has broadened my understanding and awareness of the hardship that many Indigenous people still face today. The course has also energized and excited me towards the prospect of possibly working with some of the many fine Indigenous and non-Indigenous people I met throughout the course, towards re-educating the nation so that all can be up lifted (in particular the Indigenous Australian People). The course was just a wonderful opportunity to listen, learn, reflect, grow and be inspired– it's really ignited a passion within and given me a new sense of direction since coming back to the city.* Joel

> *Personally, this course had a profound impact on me. I greatly appreciated the opportunity to learn about Indigenous culture, people and issues, in both theory and practice. The meaningful relationships which I was*

able to make with Indigenous and non-Indigenous people, concerned about Aboriginal issues, were also very special and filled with learning and laughter. Overall, this course was an incredible experience which equipped me with knowledge, skills, and relationships and filled me with hope for the future of Aboriginal Australians. Ashleigh 2009

Ways We Have Learnt To Work With Refugees In Australia
Angie Andrews

In 1985, when I was initially employed by Baptist Community Services, I was asked to work with women and children in crisis. Later I asked if I could focus my work specifically on migrant and refugee families, particularly refugee women and children at risk.

In 1989 I established the West End Migrant and Refugee Support Group (or "Refugee Support Group") and since then, have acted as Coordinator of the Refugee Support Group which facilitates a continuous flow of volunteers who are committed to supporting newly arrived refugees settling in West End, Hill End, Highgate Hill, South Brisbane, East Brisbane, Annerley, Buranda, Coorparoo, Greenslopes, Moorooka, Stones Corner and Woolloongabba.

A major part of my responsibility as the Coordinator of the Refugee Support Group has been to recruit, organise, train and supervise volunteers to work with refugees.

Recruiting volunteers to work with refugees is particularly difficult for a number of reasons. Firstly, only one in eight of those who offer to help are actually likely to be of help. Secondly, 80% of those who really want to help, don't usually want to help for more than three months. Yet, because of the discontinuity most refugees have gone through, I have learnt that it is really important to ask volunteers to commit to at least a year's continuous involvement with a refugee or refugee family.

Angie is a follower of the nonviolent Jesus. She was raised in a Greek community and lived in an Indian community. She is married to Dave, with two daughters Vonny and Navi, two sons-in-law Marty and Geyan, and two grandchildren Lila and Kaedin. She supports refugees in all aspects of settlement, creating employment options with marginalized groups.

Finding good quality volunteers who have a good grasp of cross–cultural communication and the issues facing newly arrived refugees takes quite a good deal of time. I recruit volunteers from universities, seminaries and churches often through the Community Orientation Course. I run a seminar on working with refugees as a core part of the Orientation Course.

I have developed a large network of volunteers to work with refugees. At any one time there are 20 to 25 volunteers actively involved in assisting the Refugee Support Group.

I supervise these volunteers individually by meeting them regularly, encouraging them to develop a sense of vocation in their work (whether it is paid or unpaid) and helping them learn some of the complexities involved in inter-faith, cross-cultural, community work with often seriously traumatised refugees families. The Refugee Support Group has fulfilled many refugee support functions.

Advocacy

The Refugee Support Group has always advocated for vulnerable Asylum Seekers with the Friends of Edmund and the Refugee Claimant Centre. In fact the Refugee Claimant Centre started at The House Centre at 69 Thomas Street West End, which has a long association with the Waiters Union.

We have provided accommodation, employment and support for refugee claimants; and – in a number of celebrated cases – with the help of volunteer lawyers like Peter Noble, have successfully fought against their wrongful deportation.

Airfares

The Refugee Support Group partnered with a range of stakeholders (including TEAR Australia and its volunteer committee in Queensland, Community Initiatives Resource Association, local ethnic communities and donors) to help establish and maintain the Refugee Airfare Loans scheme (RALS).

The purpose of RALS is to provide Humanitarian Entrants who would not otherwise be able to pay for their airfare, with access to a loan without interest and a repayment plan tailored to suit the applicant's financial circumstances.

The loans scheme is not simply a credit facility for airfares, it is a community-based initiative to assist refugees to settle in Australia. The purpose of having a "revolving loan scheme" is to maximise the capital available to assist people. This gives recipients an opportunity to assist the "next generation" of people in need.

Since it started RALS has assisted about 100 refugees in coming to Australia – and there has not been a single default in the repayments of loans.

Settlement

Ensuring the safe arrival of refugees from refugee camps around the world begins with a series of lengthy, detailed negotiations with the relevant government departments. These negotiations may take a long, long time – anything from one to six years for each case.

Immediate settlement involves welcoming refugees. Upon being advised by the Immigration Department of their imminent arrival, we need to be ready to go to the airport at any time – day or night – to greet the refugees.

Immediate settlement also involves providing accommodation for the refugees. So we need to have arranged accommodation for them upon their arrival. This means accessing housing through immigration housing complexes, general real estate agents or government funded housing agencies such as Brisbane Boarders or MATCH Housing.

Short term settlement involves linking refugees to the welfare, education and health systems. Typically, we settle the refugees in their short-term housing one day and the next working day take them to Centrelink to sort out their benefits and ensure rental payments to the respective housing bodies. Then we take adults to TAFE to sign them up for English classes and take the children to Milperra State High School for special transitional classes to help them adjust to Australian school education. Last but not least, we take the new arrivals to get health checks – for tuberculosis and other common contagious diseases.

Medium term settlement involves linking refugees to networks of support, personal friends and personalised care. We usually introduce a refugee to a volunteer who visits them regularly and ensures they have the support that they need. Typically, they start by helping meet an obvious felt need, such as assisting with English as a Second Language (ESL) training with illiterate refugees or assisting literate adults and children with homework. But these volunteers don't just help with homework, they take an active interest in the family itself and – wherever possible – assist them with any difficulties they are facing. For example, they may go to the local school that the children attend and may help iron out any misunderstandings the children or the parents may be having with the school authorities. If the children are bored, they may arrange extracurricular activities such as music or sport. If the parents are traumatised, they may arrange regular visits to a clinic for victims of torture.

Long term settlement involves linking refugees to appropriate work, appreciative church and affirmative culture options. We have always been interested in organising appropriate employment options for refugees, including placing people individually in jobs and setting up job collectives. Previously we negotiated a recruiting and training pathway for refugees into employment with church-based aged-care facilities. Many of the volunteers have helped refugees connect with their churches and helped their churches include refugees. Annerley Baptist, Centenary Baptist, Gateway Baptist, Kenmore Baptist, and Windsor Road Baptist are all churches that have been appreciative of their association with refugees and have been appreciated by refugees. We encourage people to avoid disassociation on the one hand and assimilation on the other – and to work towards affirmation of the best of both the resident and refugee cultures.

Resources

For 15 years we had a resource collection point located under our house. The collection point acted as a recycling unit for people who wanted to pass on used household items to newly arrived refugee families. We always had enough goods under the house to completely set up a family with everything they would need to start up a home.

We would receive donations from churches, such as Gateway Baptist. We would then sort out the contributions, keeping the quality goods and discarding the junk. We would wash all the linen and utensils and stack them together neatly in nice colour co-ordinated lots. When a new family arrived we would take the best lot we had and give it to them.

Groups

We ran a Torture and Trauma Support Group in our home for four years until Queensland Program of Assistance to Survivors of Torture and Trauma (QPASTT) was established.

Then we ran an Inter-Faith Dialogue Group for refugees in our home for two years, exploring topics such as racism, compassion and forgiveness and how God related to these issues in their lives. We also ran a Study Group in our home for two years for refugees interested in exploring the Gospel more deeply by reading and discussing *Not Religion But Love*.

At one time we also ran a popular multi-cultural One World Music Group in our home.

But of all the groups, probably the most well known is the famous Refugee Sewing Group that has been running for 20 years – and is still running. We started the Sewing Group to create a safe meeting space that would break down the barriers between Australians and new arrivals, give refugee women a chance to speak English in a non-threatening environment and learn to sew cheap, culturally appropriate clothes for their families. Many of the friendships that started in the Sewing Group continue to this day.

Co-operatives

We have supported a range of co-operative initiatives over the years.

Marty Richards started Ethical Pest Management (EPM), with the help of Marc Blum and Brett Hunter, to provide employment for refugees whose qualifications weren't recognised in Australia. Marty manages EPM with Ali Karimi, an Afghan agriculturalist who fled to Australia as a refugee and now is a qualified pest controller.

Wendy Moore started a Cooking Co-op to generate income for a few refugee women. Wendy and her team of refugee women prepared a range of quality three-course gourmet meals and delivered them freshly-made to their customers' homes when ordered.

We assisted Saba Abraham in establishing a Mobile Food Service which caters for large government and non-government agency events by providing great traditional Eritrean food. The Mobile Food Service, employing 25 members of the Eritrean Women and Family Support Network, has been able to put Eritreans on the map in Australia; make Eritrean food and beverages available to the wider Brisbane community; provide the Brisbane community with an experience of Eritrean culture; introduce people to the famous traditional Eritrean coffee ceremony which uses time-honoured preparation and presentation techniques; interact as Eritrean–Australians with other Australians – creating a positive cross-cultural experience and sharing a culture of hospitality; and assisting their youth in settling more effectively in Australia by encouraging pride in their own culture and acceptance of people from other cultures. Through the Mobile Food Service, the Eritrean Women and Family Support Network say they have been able to get much needed work experience; acquire catering knowledge and skills; access opportunities to enhance language; develop a sense of confidence and self-reliance; discover a sense of their "place" in the wider society; contribute their traditional culinary skills to the broader community; and engage the Brisbane community more effectively. They now run their own restaurant in Moorooka called Mu'ooz.

Most recently Judy Collins-Haynes and I, with the help of a whole team of hardworking volunteers, transformed the Sewing Group into an income generating project. We called it westendnetwork.com to indicate that it was meant to be a network that would support a range of social enterprises we are involved with – generating employment with our friends from refugee backgrounds. To begin with we didn't get much of a response. We would get up at 4.00 am and work through to 4.00 pm, selling products at local markets and only make $150. It was totally unviable. However, as you know, like the women I work with, I am not the kind of person to give up easily. So we kept going to the markets until we managed to find venues that would give the women a better return on their labour. Eventually we discovered conferences and festivals. We can sell 500 of the bags the women make at a conference and make $1500 a day at a festival – 10 times what we were making at the market. So business is booming. And are the women happy about that? Just look and see for yourselves at www.new.facebook.com/video/video.php? v=31288596166&oid=5560742993.

•

When times get tough and I wonder about the significance of our work I always remember what Kebreab Abraham, a past Chairman of the Eritrean Community Association said, "I have known Ange (since) 1996 when I was desperate for help. The help and care I have received from the West End Migrant and Refugee Support Group was so great that I cannot find the words to explain my feelings. Without their help, many of us would not be (here in Australia) in the position we are now (in). *The (Support Group) is our second home.*"

2010

A National Park For Aussie Christians
Lin Hatfield Dodds

I have been an enthusiastic supporter of the Waiters Union for nearly 15 years. My partner and I participated in a Waiters Union community development course entitled "With Christ in the Community" in the very early 90s.

- The daily program started with prayer.

- After breakfast we joined in studies.

- People shared of their life in the local community involving peace networks, community arts, housing assistance, legal aid, refugee resettlement, and offering hospitality and shelter to those without a place to stay.

- The afternoons were unstructured times to allow us to get to know the neighbourhood and its people.

- In the evenings we had dinner with different members of the network.

- Most days finished with a much-needed debriefing session.

- We also managed to squeeze in time to deliver meals on wheels, go on outings with people who had intellectual disabilities and help out at an evening meal for over a hundred homeless men.

- The nine of us on the course lived in a group house for the first week, moving out to stay in boarding houses or

---

Lin wants to change the world. Like many Waiters Union members and friends, she works where she is with the resources to hand. She is a member of the Uniting Church, serves on a range of boards and has received several awards for her contribution to the community. She is the National Director of Uniting Care Australia. She lives in Canberra with her partner Steve and two teenage sons.

hostels we found for ourselves in the second week.

- For many of us this was a difficult and sometimes frightening experience, living in the midst of depressed and often violent lives, and it was good to come back together for the last few days to the security of group living.

Highlights of the course for us included:

- meeting people who not only talk about being compassionate, but who are trying to put these things into practice

- developing friendships

- hearing people's stories, and

- being involved in a Murri service in a maximum security prison.

The quality of our experiences, the relationships that developed and that continue to nurture and encourage us, and the opportunity to reflect at the nexus of theology and real world practice shaped our lives in profound ways through our twenties and thirties and into our forties. Our experience I know is not at all unusual.

I believe that the Waiters Union contributes directly and indirectly to the wider life of the church and has a significant role as a living alternative to "mainstream" Australian Christian community.

The Waiters Union contributes directly to the wider life *of* the church.

I believe that the Waiters Union makes an extremely significant contribution to the life and mission of the Christian church in

Australia. This contribution goes well beyond Queensland.

I am a national leader in the life of the Uniting Church in Australia, and have often noted Waiters Union folk contributing to significant events in the life of the church: For example, someone from the Waiters Union delivered an inspiriting keynote address at the Uniting Church of Australia's National Theological Consultation several years ago that significantly influenced the culture of the consultation in a very positive way. Several influential books have come out of the Waiters Union community that have reached and influenced a wide audience across the church in Australia.

The Waiters Union nurtures radical disciples and visionary leaders *for* the church.

The Waiters Union breeds radical discipleship, based on the visionary agenda of Christ and grounded in the real life experience and hard won wisdom in the Waiters Union community of friends. It grows leadership rooted in a soul deep yearning to respond to God's call to participate in transforming the lives of individuals, families and communities. It's a living example of courage and risk and holiness to all who connect with it, as a group of ordinary Aussies do their best to live out the costly, risky business of being part of God's movement in our world in a pretty ordinary urban environment.

The Waiters call us by living example to visit the sick or imprisoned, give someone thirsty a drink, or volunteer to drive the local community bus to pick up people living with disability. They remind us that God calls us to integrity and congruence, that in every daily decision we can choose to enact hope and grace and service or not. And they do this in the same sorts of suburbs that most of us live in. That's the real challenge. How easy is it to hear stories of discipleship and mission from other countries and how challenging to experience them on our doorsteps in the same environments that we live in ourselves.

The Waiters Union is a beacon of hope for many who feel disenfranchised *by* the church.

The Waiters don't have formal structures, they have never incorporated, they don't prepare annual reports with profit and loss statements. They are a movement rather than an organization and as such I believe are able to move with God's Spirit in ways that more organized entities simply cannot.

They are a breath of fresh air for many of us. The National Church Life Survey tells us the current institutions of the church in the developed West are in trouble. They are less relevant, less engaging to ordinary Australians than in previous decades. I believe that as churches we have a responsibility to nurture different expressions of faith community, now more than ever.

Certainly, the Waiters Union is a fairly unique expression of faith community. I have participated in Sunday worship services in West End where I have been ministered to by people living with schizophrenia, who are homeless, or struggling with addictions to alcohol or other drugs. These people have not just been welcomed into the life of this vibrant community of faith, they have been offered opportunities to contribute and their contributions have been valued.

I could not state strongly enough the life giving hope for many of us around Australia to know that in Brisbane, the Waiters Union are doing their best to be faithful to their call from God. Many times as I travel across the country I meet people who have a connection to the Waiters and we often laugh and say that for those of us whose vocation lies elsewhere, the Waiters are a bit like a National Park – we can't always be there, but our past and present connection gives life to our soul and courage to choose the risky way of Christ when everything else is pushing for safety.

2005

A Safe Place For Radical Conversations
Charles Ringma

It is a cold Brisbane July Saturday morning. The kind of morning when one might be tempted to stay in bed for a while. But a small group of brave souls are already inside the Thomas Street house in West End as I make my way up the creaky stairs of the old house whose walls have been the ears to years of conversation about community, justice, peace and social transformation issues.

I can hear voices inside and smell the coffee.

I join in with the chatting before the group of some twenty people settle comfortably in the next room. Some prefer the floor. Others occupy chairs in a circle that forms as if on command. A circle that speaks of equality and commonality. A circle where all can be seen, and all will be heard.

An initiative of the Waiters Union led by Aaron Nebauer, run for many years under the gentle and pastoral leadership of Neil Barringham, Project Hope provides a monthly space for the church's radicals and "refugees" to find a place where topics that don't seem to be on the church's radar screen can be discussed with enthusiasm, passion and respect.

Today, a couple who are running a farm and are employing young people in trouble with the law and people who are newcomers to Australia, are sharing their life's journey of faith, challenges and difficulties and the unfolding of the story of their return to the land, care for God's earth, issues of financial sustainability,

---

Charles worked for nearly twenty years in serving street people and drug addicts in Brisbane. He served as a mission theologian in the Philippines and is Emeritus Professor of Mission Studies, Regent College. He continues to teach part time in Asia. One of his recent books is *The Seeking Heart: A Journey with Henri Nouwen*.

building community, providing employment, caring for the weak and journeying with the church as best as they can.

It's a story that allows many in the group to join in to the extensive conversation. All in the room – despite a diversity of ages, jobs and church affiliations – are wrestling with similar issues. How can we be the followers of Jesus today? What does it mean to be a servant and witness to the Reign of God? How can we be more ecologically sensitive? How do we care for the neighbour and the stranger? How do we serve the poor? How can we live a more simple lifestyle? And what about income generation? And how do we hang in with the church which so often seems to be so self-focused.

The topics are different each month and the speakers are from many spheres of life. We hear from missionaries doing the hard yards of incarnational ministry in the slums of New Delhi. We wrestle with living the Sermon on the Mount. We talk about just investments. We deal with biblical perspectives on economics. There is a discussion on inter-faith dialogue. A meeting deals with the relationship between intentional Christian community and the institutional church. Sexuality and spirituality is the focus of one gathering. And there are the frequent themes of what it means to follow Christ today, to be peacemakers, to act justly and to serve the poor no matter what the topic.

Saturday meetings begin with people introducing themselves and sharing a little of where they are at or the issues they are concerned about. Input from speakers usually lasts about thirty minutes and then there is discussion. The beauty of what follows is that there is both some guidance to focus on the issues of the talk and the generosity of some digression.

People who come are in the main on the periphery of the church. They feel that the church has not provided a good place for them in that discussion is not what the church does – it only teaches. Moreover, people who attend Project Hope do not believe that many churches have the right focus and priorities. They see the church as self-focused and institutionally oriented. And that the concerns of the Kingdom of God, the passion for justice, the building of community, and the concern for the planet are not strongly in focus in many churches.

It is not hard to identify why Project Hope continues to be such a good space for those who come. For many this regular gathering is the only place where they are part of a group of like-minded people. They love the meeting's diversity. They appreciate the concern to live the Christian life in a more integrated and wholistic way. They warmly welcome that in this place the hard questions of life and faith can be asked.

In so many ways Project Hope reflects what the Waiters Union seeks to be about. With a flat leadership structure, with a commitment to neighbourhood and neighbourliness, with a desire to live the gospel, with a vision to follow Christ, and with a passion to care for the vulnerable ones in our society, Project Hope resonates with the heartbeat of the Waiters Union.

While Project Hope longs for the church to create similar safe places for discussion, reflection and challenge, it will continue to act as a small signpost. Against the tide of power structures that exclude, Project Hope provides an inclusive space. Against the values of the dominant consumer culture, this meeting provides a space to reflect on a different way to live.

Small and vulnerable this monthly gathering of old and young in an old West End house is hardly a power player in the machinations of the city of Brisbane and in the mainline denominations. But it is a gift and a place of hope.

It is nearly midday and I am back on the street in the warm sunshine. But the gathering is still with me. It will be for many days to come. So many things to ponder. How can we create jobs for the poor? How can we become more connected to the land and care for it? How can we be sustained in all we seek to do in following Jesus? How can we play a part in renewing the life of the church? How can a more peaceful and just society come in to being?

Who knows what seeds of the Kingdom of God may germinate from this motley gathering?

2010

A Reference Point For Radical Christians
Greg Gow

"What is the Waiters Union?" How to answer that question? At least among most I know in Melbourne nobody can confidently explain what constitutes the Waiters Union. It is marvelous how the fragile Waiters Union with all its lack of clarity has profoundly impacted so many lives (including my own) over such a long period. I cannot explain the magic of it, all I know is that hundreds of us thank God for the Waiters.

In what follows I endeavour to sketch something of how the Waiters Union based in Brisbane has influenced the formation of a range of Jesus-centred enterprises in Melbourne. As I hope to show, the Waiters Union has profoundly influenced the shaping of various radical Christian enterprises across Melbourne over the past 18 years.

Flashback 1992. West End, Brisbane. The Waiters Union Community Orientation Course completed over two weeks. I was a 25 year old Youth Pastor in Melbourne. My wife Rose and I travelled together up to Brisbane. We travelled back changed people who quickly encouraged others to participate in the course. Meanwhile, we purchased multiple copies of the book *Can You Hear the Heartbeat* (which describes many of the ideas advocated in the course) and began giving them away. In turn, *Can You Hear the Heartbeat* became an authoritative voice among the youth in our own North Blackburn Uniting Church youth community.

By 1993 young people from Blackburn started regularly travelling up to Brisbane to spend time in West End, participate in the Waiters Union course, and in some instances live in the

---

Greg Gow was born in Melbourne and is a pastor with Footscray Church of Christ where he now resides. He is married with three children.

Waiters' Bristol Street community house on Boundary Street. Long term relationships were formed. At least among the Blackburn crew, it was the 1998 marriage of Martin Richards (a key leader in the Blackburn Community Network) to Evonne Andrews (West End long termer) which solidified these ties. By then a group of us had relocated to Footscray in Melbourne's west and a Footscray/West End nexus was formed.

The Waiters Union Course came at an important time for us in Melbourne. It was a gift from God in the early 1990s to many of us who wanted to follow Christ in radical ways but could not find a church or organizational base from which to operate. In my view the Waiters Union particularly spoke to Generation X Christians. The Waiters purveyed a wonderful marriage of anarchism and radical Christianity which was just right for us at the time.

In Melbourne during the 1970s and 1980s there was a smorgasbord of church-based intentional Christian communities who sought to practise radical discipleship together. There was also a range of forums where people would gather to discuss ideas and spur one another on. Among others there were The House of the Gentle Bunyip Community, the Westgate Baptist Church, St Kilda Baptist Church, the Prophet's Pulpit series, Strength to Love conferences, Dallas Community, St Martins Community Church, Truth Liberation Concern and God's Squad. In the 1980s TEAR Australia also emerged in the Melbourne context.

The "radical discipleship" catchcry marked these endeavours which featured various strong heroic leaders such as John Smith, John Uren, Athol Gill and later Tim Costello. These endeavours were driven by the Baby Boomers' desire to wed evangelism and social justice. Books such as *Call to Conversion* by Jim Wallis spoke to this generation during the 1970s and 80s. By the early 1990s some of these enterprises continued but some had lost momentum, imploded or closed down.

I mention heroic leaders, because at the time Generation Xers like myself were typically suspicious of leaders. We did not want a hero leader to follow and we felt a lack of affinity with the Baby Boomer radical discipleship agendas. Concurrently, we had lost interest in church as we knew it. Yet we wanted to follow Christ.

The Waiters was not an organization, it was certainly not a church. It did not have membership, nor did it have a hero leader. It seemed nobody in particular led it. This was inconceivable to us. We had never seen it before. And we loved it. Enough that we wanted to replicate it. We tried, but soon realized we could not be as anarchistic as the Waiters. The Union is indigenous to and a metonym of West End, Brisbane. It was not a franchise. We in Melbourne had to find our own way by making the Waiters a reference point but not our goal.

We set about doing this, first in leafy Blackburn (1992–94), then later in grungy Footscray (1995 and current). The Blackburn Community Network (BCN) was sparked by lessons taken from the Waiters Union. A network of radicalized middle class youth committed to economic sharing and serving the poor in their own eastern suburbs locale. People from this network then fed into the shaping of UNOH (Urban Neighbourhoods Of Hope) in the mid 1990s and later Urban Seed.

By the late 1990s there seemed to be a collective conversation among young radical Christians in Melbourne about the Waiters Union. Especially people were discovering the

Waiters Union through *Can You Hear the Heartbeat*. For instance, at St Hilary's Anglican Church in Kew various young people were drawn to the amalgam of Anarchism and Christianity[10] and began travelling to West End. The Collins Street Baptist Church Urban Mission Unit (later morphing into Urban Seed) was a hub of ideas and various interns living in Central House travelled up to participate in the Community Orientation Course.

Many of us in radical Christian circles in Melbourne have been prone to a kind of radical Christian triumphalism. We have been so proud of our own particular radical Christian agendas to change the world that, from time to time, you could put a bunch of radicalised Christians together in one room and you could end up with a war on your hands! The Brisbane crew has appealed to many of us because they offered us a more unpretentious, less competitive understanding about what being a radical Christian involves. The Brisbane credo, "do little things with a lot of love over the long haul" is so much more sustainable.

Flashforward 2010. I am now approaching middle age and still following Christ. I thank God I am not angry and embittered. I have returned to church. In fact I am now a church pastor in Footscray. With God's help I have kept going. I have kept my sanity and most relationships intact. I am no longer driven by competitiveness but – I hope – by kindness.

The blessings of Waiters I carry with me and I know many of my Melbourne peers do likewise – remember, "there is no salvation without grace and no grace without suffering".

2010

---

[10] For an exploration of the concept of Christian Anarchism, see Jim Dowling and Anne Rampa "The Waiters Union and Christian Anarchy" which follows.

The Waiters Union And Christian Anarchy
Jim Dowling and Anne Rampa

We come from a Catholic Worker tradition, where anarchism is an integral part. We have also been part of the wider Waiters Union network since its beginnings.

For most Christians the word anarchism has only negative connotations, but just as there seem to be many interpretations of how to live a Christian life, so anarchism is open to all sorts of variations.

For us Christianity and anarchy came together firstly when Cain asked God the all-important question, "Am I my brother's keeper?" (Gen. 4:9). For Christians the answer is a clear "Yes".

God tells the Israelites what a disaster it will be if they become like other nations and appoint a "king" as their "keeper". The king will take their sons and daughters and make them work for him and his officials, that they will become enslaved to him, and that they will cry to Yahweh because of the king they have chosen, "but on that day Yahweh will not hear you" (1 Sam. 8: 7–22).

This may seem a different situation to the one we have here in Australia, because we have the power to elect new leaders on a regular basis, although in theory we still do have a "queen". But our enslavement to this system deserves a closer examination and our passing of our Christian responsibility for others onto the government is obvious. The Israelites wanted a king to "rule us and lead us and fight our battles" (1 Sam. 8:5). They no

---

Jim and Ann are both born and bred Brisbanites. They have seven children, and are living at the moment on a farm north of Brisbane, making vegetarian soap, and continuing on in their lifestyle of voluntary simplicity, nonviolent direct action against violence, and lots of other bits and pieces to hopefully help build "a new society in the shell of the old".

longer wanted or trusted God to do so – and we are no different today. We would argue that instead of a "king" we are ruled by the more abstract tyrant of modern capitalism, embodied in the "businessman". Peter Maurin, co-founder of the Catholic Worker movement wrote, "Modern society has separated the Church from the State, but it has not separated the State from business. Modern society does not believe in a Church's State; it believes in a businessmen's State. And it's the first time in the history of the world that the State is controlled by businessmen".

Now that economics directs our lives, instead of God, we accept the giving of a monetary value to everything we do. What is given the least monetary value but the care and companioning of the old, young, sick, imprisoned, and poor – the very ones to whom Christ directs us in order to be involved with Him. Jesus told us clearly that we can't serve God and money, and a system that is set up to make money for us will inevitably lead us away from our God.

A Christian anarchist chooses God, as revealed to us in the life and words of Jesus, to be our "ruler". Much inspiration for this comes from the Beatitudes. The repeated reading of the Beatitudes converted the hard-nosed atheist anarchist, Ammon Hennacy, to Christianity and it will convert us too – away from violence and towards poverty, gentleness, compassion, purity, seeking after justice and peace. It will help us joyfully accept derision and conflict that comes our way because we are always working and living "against the tide" when we seek the Kingdom of God.

The Waiters Union embraced this radical new direction towards God by firstly looking for the needs around us which we could help meet, then caring for and companioning those people without any concern for monetary input.

We were quickly plunged into the issue of the displacement of the poor in our neighbourhood, because of Expo '88. We organised ways to confront that personally and politically in a campaign that involved prayer, fasting, picketing, rallies, and rewarding landlords that resisted the temptation to make money from the situation. The media were invited to come and celebrate our efforts with us. It was very successful and there have been the flow on effects of preserving and building homes for the poor in the inner city, where services are more available to those without transport of their own.

As a community, we were already offering a home to those in need of accommodation. We shared their lives and struggles without payment from government or church. When the Waiters Union was formed, we felt a kinship immediately with these other people gathered to serve Christ in the poor at a "personal cost" and found mutuality, support and fellowship with them.

We have had the luxury of enjoying the relationships, distributing information, and generally fitting in where we could while having very little to do with the day-to-day practicalities of organising and housekeeping. We avoided decision-making on direction and organisation, but of course we are not alone in this. There was no compulsion to take a part in anything which no doubt caused frustration for those organising. We have contributed very little to the financial running of the Waiters Union (mea culpa!).

However, close association with the Bristol Street house began. This house was a community house of (mostly) young people associated with Waiters Union, experimenting with living together, and serving one another and the poor of West End. We swapped prayers, insights, guests, stories, tears, and laughter. An-archy means "without rulers". If one believes in a sacred equality of all people, and not in a system of some having power over others, then it seems the only way to survive is to love one another, to serve one another, to "wait on" one another, as the name "Waiters Union" implies. Anarchism becomes not an act of angry rebellion but an awesome acceptance of personal responsibility – for one another and the world around us.

For us it also intrinsically includes the rejection of any sort of violence as a means to try and solve our problems. This means we resist our society's obsession with "violent solutions" in the waging of war, provision of abortion services, and other more subtle forms of violence such as racism. We confront these in a variety of ways, including nonviolent direct action, which could end in arrest and imprisonment, and sometimes has. Without a supportive network like the Waiters Union around us it would have been so much harder to maintain this level of resistance, especially as we began to have children.

Does the Waiters Union function as some ideal of anarchist organising or Christian living? Very few, possibly none, of those involved over the years would answer, "Yes".

We watched from the sidelines the inevitable fights over power and direction of the Waiters Union. (We often experienced similar conflicts in our own small community.) We have remained good friends both with people who have left the Waiters Union very bitter over these issues, as well as those still there. The truth is the Waiters Union has not always functioned as a perfect model of anarchy or of Christianity.

However, our most common observation has been that many of the complaints about "power," have involved a desire for "perceived power" without a corresponding desire to take on all the responsibility it entails. We have never felt that space has not been given for us to speak or act. At the same time, being the flawed humans we are, there is little doubt that some of the criticism of those "in power" is valid.

Generally however, we would say the Waiters Union has functioned as a group with the most amazing amount of egalitarianism in terms of respect for one another. Perhaps from an underlying philosophy of respect for the marginalised, there seems to be little room for elitism in day-to-day relationships.

The Waiters Union has often embraced some of the most marginalised people from hostels or refugee camps and put them at the centre of community living. Not just eliminating a society where the leaders "lord it over others" as Jesus warned the disciples against (Matt. 20: 24–28), but building a society where those with little power or respect from society can have a voice.

In doing this we have often seen in the Waiters Union the beautiful and moving reality of Christian anarchism at work.

2010

The Waiters Union And The Traditional Church
Craig Mischewski

I have observed the Waiters Union since 1986 and was associated with them in 2001-02 through participating in the Community Orientation Course and maintaining my relationship with people in the network after the course while I was based in Brisbane.

It is my observation that the Waiters Union plays a vital role in the life of the church. The Waiters Union serves the church through serving the community in intentional Christian practices such as equitable living, acts of justice, mercy and compassion. They provide a prophetic vision to the Church through their engagement of alternative economic models, which reflect something of God's economic model of salvation. Their simple, uncompromising and generous acts of love resemble God's acts of love to us revealed in Grace, which is essentially an act of evangelisation, that is, it brings the good news of salvation to us. There is no doubt that their models of doing church may seem disconnected from more conventional models of church, but they are nonetheless effective for the culture that they have been called by God to serve with the Gospel.

The ministry of the Waiters Union continues to be inspirational to many. They offer a ray of hope to those of us who struggle with the institutionalisation of church and find that they cannot feel connected to more popular models of church. This is by no means a condemnation of the "traditional" church in its more conventional outworking, it is simply a recognition of what is

---

Craig is a minister at Townsville Central City Mission. He is married to Jude and they have seven children, two grandchildren, plus a few ring-ins. Craig has a background in community development, in particular family support and youth support. One of his great passions in life is fishing and camping trips.

a reality for many folk.

What's the traditional church? I guess the place to start is a definition of "traditional." Traditional comes from the Latin word "traditio" which means to hand over or pass on.

When we look around at what has been handed on as traditional church, we see gothic buildings, brick god boxes, 1970s brick veneer, sloping roof, cross laden structures and very large school hall type buildings, designed to hold thousands of people.

All of these "traditional" structures conjure up for the majority of middle earth Australians an image of people sitting or standing in rows, singing, praying or just looking at the back of the head of the person in front of them. Which is, of course, pretty much what happens.

There are some very funny cultural stereotypes that go with this image shaped and supported by comedians like Dick Emery, Rowan Atkinson and the Two Ronnies, of conservative men quoting Scripture and appeasing the flower arranging guild as in Keeping Mum. But for many, church business is serious business, after all people have killed each other over it.

My experience is that it is about a group of people who get together because they believe in God and agree with each other about how that belief should be lived out, thought about and articulated. These folk know that what they believe and do is right because the people who were in charge of the church before them believed the same thing, and there you have it, it must be right. Thus we get the "traditional" church.

The Waiters Union? Not a gothic, god box, cross laden building or anything resembling a facility to house the orthodox belief of the faithful. How then is the "traditional" church to relate and understand it?

First, it's a movement and a network, which is pretty hard to tie down and pigeon hole. Second, it doesn't seem to have a faith statement so one cannot determine its orthodoxy. Very confusing and a little scary. Because many of the network identify with Jesus of Nazareth, the Lord of the Church, the traditional church feels there should be some sort of relationship, but doesn't know how to define the Waiters Union and therefore doesn't know how to relate to the Waiters Union.

History shows that because the Waiters Union has not slipped easily between the sheets of traditional church understanding, the church has struggled to find a point of contact, and perhaps has struggled to find a value application so as to determine the safety of any real relationship.

The Waiters Union does not exist to put bums on pews, they don't wave the banner of any particular denomination nor do they engage in acts of gratuitous proselytisation for the Christian Church (a problem for some).

The traditional church tends toward an industrialised approach to the coming of the Kingdom of Heaven. People must be converted, which is often secret code for "they must become like us." There is a major and continued effort put into sustaining or growing each of the church communities and keeping the buildings in pristine condition.

Please do not think that I believe that the traditional church has no value. The church is full of many heroes and heroines of faith. Those who pray long into the night for their communities, those who serve their neighbour counting any sacrifice as a great honour and those who joyfully share their resources with the poor of this world. Many a good person has been formed in the traditional church, just look around the Waiters Union!

In 2007 the Uniting Church in Australia (UCA) in Queensland established a three year relationship with some of the Waiters involved in training, under the umbrella of Vision for Mission, an outreach and education strategy of the UCA. This relationship revolved around the team of trainers providing consultation and education with regard to Christian community development. The expectation was that these workers would make themselves and their skills/knowledge available to pass onto traditional church folk, who then attempt to morph that into their local context.

I think herein lies a healthy relationship between the Waiters Union and the traditional church. The Waiters Union has learned that the Kingdom of Heaven comes to Earth when people form right relatedness that empowers and inspires a culture of love, honour and generosity. It is in the midst of this cultural osmosis that the risen Lord Jesus is best expressed and experienced through hearts and hands of very ordinary people with an extraordinary ambition toward building a better world.

The traditional church has the capacity to connect with a really big group of people. If there is a healthy and synergetic relationship between the Waiters Union and the traditional church, then together, we can pass on a really powerful message; "God loves you, stop hurting each other and let God show you a better way." The Waiters Union is a network of likeminded people with a vision for a better world; the traditional church is a large organisation with a mandate to share God's love for the world. It could be a match made in Heaven. 2010

The Waiters Union And the Emerging Church
Steve Drinkall

Several years ago, I found myself outside of the traditional church.

I had previously worked as a youth pastor at a local suburban church and must admit that I really enjoyed it. My particular skills and outlook were perfectly suited to the traditional church set up and I found a lot of affirmation and a modest amount of success in what I was doing.

This all changed when I left the staff of the church in order to spend more time performing with the rock band that I had formed with my brother. For a while I still attended a local church, however, a combination of touring and weekend work saw the gap between me and church widen. I was still enthusiastic about following Jesus, however, for the first time in my life I started to see my local church from an outsider's perspective.

I began to wonder if my musician friends would ever want to come to the kind of church that we attended and I began to doubt that they would. Was there a way for them to encounter God without first attending a church service? These and other questions have occupied my mind for most of the last ten years and have led me on a path of trying to work out what it looks like to be an authentic follower of Jesus in our time and in our city.

After a while I decided that my friends and I were trying to work out the answers to these questions largely on our own. I decided to go and look for other likeminded people or groups, who were

---

Steve has spent the last 15 years trying to work out what is means to follow Jesus in our contemporary society as well as experimenting with ways forward for the church into the future. Steve is a musician, youth worker and public speaker. He lives in Brisbane, Australia with his wife and two kids.

in our area and who were further down this journey than we were. I figured that we could benefit from their insights and maybe even work together on a few things.

I asked around my networks and my friend mentioned that a fellow called Dave had been involved with a Christian community in West End called the "Waiters Union" and that the group had been running for quite a few years.

I must admit that I didn't quite know what to expect but I rang him and booked a time to go to West End and pick his brains. When I arrived at the coffee shop, I immediately recognized Dave as the lecturer I had had years before while doing some youth work study. I had also known of Dave Andrews through his involvement with TEAR Australia and his work in the area of social justice but I had never much thought of him as a church kind of guy. He welcomed me and I began to explain why I had come to see him.

As I poured out my story about trying to start something new and about how the church is missing the mark in terms of connecting with the community and how we need a radical rethink of what church is and what it means to follow Jesus, Dave sat and patiently let me finish my rant. He then took a long sip of his coffee and decided not answer any of my questions but rather to tell me his own story and the story of the Waiters Union.

I listened intently as he explained to me that they had started out with many of the same questions as we had. How they had decided to move into the lowest socio-economic area in the city and then to work out what it means to follow Jesus in the real mess and reality of people's lives. He outlined some of the lessons that they had learned in trying to develop a community of faith in that area and shared openly about both their successes and failures along the way. I heard tales of social enterprises, advocacy on behalf of the poor, and of the church service they ran for those who wouldn't be welcome in most other church meetings.

As the story went on, Dave was constantly interrupted by local residents who passed by on the street and either said "hello" or stopped to chat. Lawyers, prostitutes, young adults, business owners, drug addicts, refugees and a range of people from all over the world.

I was struck by how embedded Dave was in the lives of the people in his community and quickly realized that here was a Christian leader who represented a community that was truly much farther down this journey than I would have imagined. A Christian community who was diligently trying to make sense of what it means to follow Jesus in the true mess of the lives of their local neighbours.

I did not get the impression that this community was in any way faultless or that they had arrived at their destination but I certainly got the feeling that this group was up and running and well on their way.

The most impressive part of the whole story for me was that they had been diligently experimenting with these ideas and faithfully trying to live them out for well over 20 years, long before anyone had used the words "emerging church."

What is the "emerging" church? This question is much harder to answer than it looks. A casual Google or Youtube search will only serve to confuse you with its polarizing views.

My take is simply this. The world is in a time of rapid change and the ground is shifting in almost every area of life. The next 30 years of change will leave no area unaffected. Economics, sport, medicine, religion, education and relationships will all look vastly different in 2040 and beyond. With that in mind it seems highly unlikely that the kind of church we will need in the future is the one we have now.

What we have now and have had for the last hundred years or so is simply not going to connect with and communicate to the world that we are heading into. The problem is that no one really knows what the church will need to be in the future. The answers are still "emerging".

The "emerging" church is not a defined group of people but rather a conversation about where to from here for followers of Jesus. It is a name given to the conglomerate of people who are packing up camp and getting back on the road in order to try and work out how we should respond in these times.

This definition fits the Waiters Union perfectly. They do not have a model that they are promoting. They are not a defined group that you can join in the traditional sense. They are not even a community but rather are a group of friends who are attempting to be "community" to each other and to build that sense of community into every corner of their neighbourhood.

The Waiters Union packed up their tents many years ago and have been doing their best to resist the temptation to set up camp again. They are the first real life example that I have seen of a community who lives the ideas of the "emerging" church movement.

I have met many others from the Waiters Union and have seen them live and operate in a variety of settings. From the outside it looks messy in that there aren't many common meetings that everyone attends or clear lines of command or accountability. It doesn't look like an organization and yet the simple structures that they do have serve their purposes well.

The Waiters are about people and they don't seek to explain themselves by sending you to their website or by mailing you their vision statement and theological beliefs. They simply invite you to come and see, to meet a few people and hang out with them for a while.

It may sound chaotic but I have found the members of the Waiters Union to be clear in their intention to transform their community and passionate and strategic in how they go about their work. They do it one life at a time and alongside each other in a way that honours the journey of each individual and that points them towards Jesus.

The Waiters Union shows us a glimpse of what things might look like for all of us in the future.

2010

The Waiters Union And Local Mission
Kenn Baker

"You've had WHAT stolen?"

This was not the only interesting conversation I participated in during a period of a little over one and a half years with members from the Waiters Union while working on a common project to provide emergency accommodation for single women in our home city of Brisbane.

A number of inner city churches signed up to provide emergency accommodation for single women in our home city of Brisbane. The Waiters Union organised for the community house that they were associated with to also become part of the vision. The idea was straightforward. There was a shortage of options for single women in need of emergency accommodation and there were church buildings in inner city Brisbane lying vacant most nights of the week. The challenge was to bring the need and the solution together: to provide a space for women to lie on mattresses in church buildings which would otherwise lie empty.

In the process there were many questions of logistics. How do we launder that many sheets and pillow cases week after week? What do we do if a male friend shows up at the location and becomes aggressive or even violent? How do we open church buildings up in a way that is friendly and welcoming so guests don't feel like they've just interacted with an institution?

As some of these questions were answered (and others were left

---

Kenn was born in Mundubbera, Queensland. He is married to Leanne and enjoys adventures with his boys, Jett who is four and Finn who is two. Kenn's interest in Jesus was piqued growing up as the son of a Methodist minister. Now, as a bi-vocational minister, this interest has led Kenn into friendships with those who are not in the church. Most recently he has led Christian faith communities in New Farm, Brisbane and Geebung, Brisbane.

in the "wait and see" category), Crash Beds was born and volunteers from all over Brisbane signed up to provide support at one of the four participating venues opened on a roster basis from Thursday through Sunday nights. Two volunteers would bunk down on freshly laundered linen and pillows and mattresses and welcomed up to six single women as guests for the night.

Along the way volunteers came with homemade delicacies, board games were unfolded, hot water flowed from showers, conversations ensued, and unlikely friendships developed.

Many of the volunteers were closely connected with the city themselves, and the project seeped outside its official Thursday through Friday night time slot. We heard stories of city professionals meeting and chatting with some of the women they chanced to meet in city streets throughout the working week.

A guest who had been sleeping rough for many years moved into government-assisted accommodation and several project volunteers were welcomed by her for an informal house warming afternoon tea. Then we were saddened together to see this woman leave her accommodation and again join us Thursday through Sunday.

As guests and volunteers became friends, volunteers started to become familiar with the complexities of problems, reasons, and pain.

Along the way there were many points of witness. Volunteers reported conversations with work colleagues, family, and friends who wanted to know what they were doing and why. Social and community development workers engaged in discussions with volunteers about how faith in Jesus related to compassionate involvement with homeless women. The women who were guests experienced the love of Christ in the care and concern of the volunteers. And, significantly, there was the witness of the volunteers to the wider church.

And along the way, Waiters provided guidance from their depth of experience to this local mission we were all having crack at. The way of the kingdom – of being a light to the nations, of offering help and assistance even to the outsider, of being known by our love, of welcoming even the little ones – is a way of mission I have seen Waiters exhibit so naturally in different contexts and at different times over these past few years.

And along the way, Waiters also etched its name into those stories of Crash Beds which are retold from time to time. Amongst the many hopeful, interesting, sad, and humorous stories which emerged from each of the four sites, this story of a car being stolen from the Waiters Union Crash Beds site seems to have made its way into the "legendary stories" annals.

However my experience of mission is that it is usually much more ordinary and much less dramatic than the "legendary stories" we tell. It often comes in the guise of small requests.

"Could you help a young guy who struggles with anxiety and depression make some friendships in your area?"

Neil Barringham, a long term participant in the Waiters Union, was looking for some good options for one of the young men he supports as part of his work with A Place To Belong.

A few months later. A few coffees later. Sitting in "the Valley." Talking with Mark. Hoping to spread hope. I sense that these times, as difficult and insignificant as they appear to be, are amongst the truest times of mission.

A friendship made.

Time spent listening.

Offering support.

Offering the gospel ... so desperately needed ... so misunderstood ... so often rejected.

An observation a friend from Waiters has recently shared came to mind: in working alongside people who are downtrodden, a difficulty we face in sharing the good news of Jesus is in helping people to believe in heaven. These friends of ours who struggle are convinced of the reality of hell; they often are living "in hell." The challenge is not to convince people of the reality of hell, it is to share with people the reality of heaven.

Mark struggles with constant anxiety. He holds down a fulltime job and maintains rent on his small apartment, but often finds himself crippled by fear and only just surviving. He feels intensely alone and sees and feels the futility and degradation of some of the destructive activities he tries in an attempt to meet his needs. At the same time he is very suspicious of the church and anyone involved in church and yet he stays in contact and we organise to have coffee together here and there. At these times, Mark has shared many of his struggles. He does not want me to pray with him while he is there, but is happy for me to pray for him in his absence.

Just recently Mark texted saying, "I'm not out of the woods yet but I will overcome."

Sitting back on a cool night, enjoying the vibes of some great local live music at the street party hosted by Blackstar Coffee as a part of the Brisbane City Council's Festival '09, Neil and I are chatting when we spot Mark amongst the crowd. Mark is at peace and obviously enjoying the music and the atmosphere of the night.

Our conversation meanders through the many interwoven friendships that have been developing in Mark's life as we piece together the snippets of stories which speak of rich interactions with people from the Waiters network. His desire was for friendship and connection and now it is hard to keep up with the connections and conversations he speaks casually about: coffee with Tom the other week, meeting up with Christel here and there, and regular attendance at a documentary night hosted by a group of common friends connected with Waiters.

My experience of mission with Waiters is hard to describe. It's almost always about connection and friendship and most often closely tied to meeting the needs of people who in one way or another are on the margins of society.

Jesus talked about the changes that would take place in the life of the person who drank deeply of the water he offers. The image Jesus' words leave is of the force of life pushing, gushing, and bubbling up, catching and reflecting light, and splashing all over whoever is standing nearby. Messy, refreshing, surprising.

This is the way of mission I have observed in my interaction with many of the people associated with the Waiters Union.

It is the way of loving people and of seeing the love of God grow within people.

It is the way of the Spirit stirring up love and life for others and catching off guard with refreshment those who come near the community of the Spirit.

It is the way of convincing people of the reality of heaven and of inviting people to live in this reality.

2010

The Waiters Union And International Mission
Mark Delaney

When Cath and I were thinking about heading to India in the early 1990s, East Timor was the big issue in justice circles in Australia. This was pre-Timorese independence. I'd seen a John Pilger documentary exposing the awful situation in Timor and the Australian government's reprehensible abandonment of the Timorese to the Indonesian military. While I hadn't personally abandoned the Timorese, I felt some responsibility for the actions of our government, from which I'd benefited much in education, healthcare and so on. So the question in 1994 for me was whether to go to India or stay in Australia and help fight for justice for the Timorese.

Cath and I had been to India as singles in the late 80s on short-terms during our university holidays. At that point, Dave and Ange Andrews had not long returned from their 12 years in India, so they had shared their wisdom, hearts and contacts in India with Cathy to help her prepare. While on those short term visits that Cath and I had taken separately, we were struck to the core by the incredible disparity between life for the poor folk we met and our own experience of middle class life in Australia. I remember meeting a man outside his "house" – a plastic tent, and hearing that his wife had just given birth to their baby days before, right there in their tent! This was December in North India – winter – when the temperatures get close to freezing. I shook hands to say goodbye. His hand felt like a block of ice! It was a simple interaction. With my limited Hindi it took perhaps only five minutes, but it was the turning point in my life. I returned to Australia with a deep sense that the world is not

---

Mark grew up in Lismore on the NSW North Coast. He and his wife Cathy both studied at the University of Queensland in the 80s. They married in 1993, joined Servants in '94 and left for Delhi in '95. They've been there ever since, with breaks every couple of years back in Brisbane.

right and an idealistic resolve to do something about it.

A couple of years later, after completing my studies and working in Brisbane, I met and fell in love with Cath. We realised quickly that we were very similar in our desire to go to the developing world, so we married in 1993 intending to get back there within a couple of years. Before subjecting ourselves to the rigors of the majority world however, we figured we'd better learn how to care for each other in the relative ease of Australia. We rented a little place in Highgate Hill for a year, during which we also started getting involved in the Waiters. After our first year, we moved into a share house with other Waiters' folk in Highgate Hill, the idea in our minds being that we should learn to be in community with others in Australia before heading overseas.

As in any community, that household was a good, yet painful year. I remember various wandering folk dropping in at any time of the day for a chat, as well as the lengthy discussions on cooking schedules, how often to eat together and so on. All simple, hair-tearing stuff. Yet, as expected, great learning too. The skills we learned there and in other communities we'd lived in; how to listen, be honest and where necessary, to confront, were to prove invaluable later in India.

Meanwhile we were also meeting with Dave Andrews once a week to discuss readings he gave us in preparation for overseas. It was an eclectic mix; Moltmann's *The Crucified God*, Schumacher's *Small is Beautiful*, Hiebert's *Anthropological Insights for Missionaries*, and Stanley Jones' *The Christ of the Indian Road*. We loved it and in retrospect are very grateful to Dave for so much time in what must have been a very busy time for him and Ange.

It was about then that East Timor became the hot topic for the justice minded in Australia. We asked Dave for his advice. He suggested that we still go to India for a couple of years while we were young and relatively unencumbered. We could make the decision about the longer-term future from there, on the basis of that experience, rather than from the relative comfort of justice work in Australia. Only in retrospect have I come to appreciate that more about the Waiters. The spirit of freeing others up to do what God is asking of them, rather than them asking folk to stay in Brisbane with the Waiters itself.

So we went to Delhi in March 1995 to experience, think and decide. We joined a group called Servants to Asia's Urban Poor (now just "Servants") whose workers attempt to live with and work with the poor in the slums of Asia's mega cities.

We moved into a poor neighbourhood in south Delhi and began to learn Hindi and to understand a little of how poverty ticks in India. We tracked down a number of Indian Christian leaders, many of whom had been involved in Dave and Ange's communities in Delhi. We asked them whether they felt there was still a place for foreigners in mission in India. Their consensus was, yes there was a place, if we were willing to work in partnership with them, the Indians, rather then come in as the expert/boss. That seemed entirely reasonable, as we certainly didn't feel like any form of development expert!

After our first couple of years we figured that we could be useful in India, so we stayed and have been here ever since! We've deliberately attempted not to set up our own projects, but rather work to encourage and equip the many committed Indian Christians working for the poor. In our own neighbourhood, we help to link our poor friends with government services like education and health care that should be available to them, but which often remain out of reach due to corruption or laziness on the government's part or simple lack of awareness or confidence on our poor friends' part.

Our two boys, Tom 13 and Oscar 8 were both born here and are doing really well. As ridiculous as it might seem, we've come to the view that a north Indian slum is actually a rich environment for raising our boys. Here they are exposed to real issues for the majority world – crowded school rooms, the rising price of flour and the ever present rats, all in a context in which we can talk together about the best response. On top of that, we also have a lot of laughs together, not least at how crazy it is that we, the introverted Australians, should be here in an incredibly crowded Muslim slum in Delhi!

When we return to Australia for a break every couple of years, we generally stay with our friends Greg and Katie in the Gabba. It's the closest thing we've got left to a home in Australia. We also find a warm welcome at the various Waiters activities: Project Hope, Men's Group, Sunday evening service at St Andrews, and, of course, Saturday morning tennis.

In these groups we find a place of acceptance from many who've had similar experiences overseas. Unlike many Australians who look to us for results, numbers and stories of God's miraculous interventions, we find in the Waiters folk a quiet understanding – a knowing that helping to bring the Kingdom in the forsaken places is usually more hard work and tears than striking results.

On the other side, when we're in India, we try to provide a place for the many folk who want to experience something of the majority world. In fact, as I write, we're looking forward to our good Waiters friends, Neil and Ben Barringham coming to spend a couple of weeks with us over Christmas. We hope and pray that a couple of weeks in an Indian slum may be as formative for them as those early community days in the Gloucester Street community house were for us. Let's see!

2010

The Waiters Union And Intentional Community
Noritta Morseu-Diop

To share my thoughts on the Waiters as a model of community, I will start at the very beginning. My experiences and long lasting relationship with the Waiters Union began when I first met Dave Andrews who was a lecturer in one of our Social Work courses at the University of Queensland in St. Lucia, Brisbane in 1988.

My first meeting with Dave then brought me into the world of the Waiters Union: groups of individuals and families who live within and nearby the West End community. Many households are in clusters near each other, across the road from each other and around the corner from each other; all of them in pursuit of a common goal.

This goal was to create better communities by first bringing individuals, families and groups in their own neighbourhood together, to care, to share and to support one another in a spirit of friendship, love, mutual respect, compassion, integrity and sincerity. By engaging their local community, they brought this message to others in the wider communities both nationally and internationally.

My involvement with the Waiters brought back many childhood memories from my own community as an Indigenous Australian woman of Torres Strait Islander heritage. I was born and raised on Tamwoy Town, Thursday Island; a small tropical island community, situated in the Torres Strait Archipelago in Far

---

Noritta is an Indigenous Australian woman from Thursday Island far north Queensland, Australia. She graduated from the School of Social Work and Social Policy in 1992 at the University of Queensland. She has worked as a social worker in grassroots communities in the areas of grief and loss, cross-cultural education, drug and alcohol rehabilitation, Indigenous health and welfare, Indigenous mental health, and the prison system. She is currently doing a Ph.D. investigating culturally appropriate ways to address the gross over-representation of Aboriginal and Torres Strait Islander People in the Australian Criminal Justice system and prisons.

North Queensland. In my community everyone looked after each other's children and if anyone caught any fish, the catch was shared amongst many families and when there was a celebratory feast, everyone was invited. Sharing and caring was a normal and natural part of island life.

Today, living in a big city and experiencing firsthand the Waiters Union's genuine love for community instills in me a sense of pride about my own island community and a feeling of hope that there are still people out there who genuinely believe in the dream of peaceful existence and respectful engagement.

I have been a Social Work Practitioner since 1992 when I completed my final year student placement with the Waiters Union. One of the things that has remained with me throughout my career was Dave's advice, which was based on the Biblical teachings of treating others as you would want to be treated. I was advised to look for the qualities in others that highlight our common humanity and similarities rather than our differences.

Dave's words to me were, "if you meet someone who looks differently from you, speaks differently from you, is dressed differently from you and you are wondering, 'how do I talk to that person?' look for our similarities as human beings. These similarities are we all get sick, we all cry when we are sad, we all want our children to be happy and healthy, focus on those things and treat the person that you are dealing with as if they were your own loved ones."

One of the core principles of the Waiters Union is about unity in diversity. I witnessed this firsthand at the wedding of Dave and Ange's daughter Evonne and son-in-law Marty. It touched my heart to see the bridal party of fifty, which consisted of people from all walks of life, different nationalities and people with disabilities. Hundreds from their local community came to the wedding and brought a dish to share.

Many of the guests were people with a psychiatric disability from various hostels surrounding West End; people that others in society would never acknowledge or consider inviting to their wedding. I felt greatly honoured when I, a mother of four, was asked to act as the chauffer for the bride and groom.

As students, Dave challenged us to "do something practical to serve the community rather than just talking about it and writing about it, put your words into action." This was during the time of the big floods in Bangladesh, where many people were left homeless and many died. Dave challenged us to do something useful to help the flood victims of Bangladesh rather than just writing an assignment about it. And fundraising we did. We had food stalls on University of Queensland Market Day, we raised awareness about the plight of the people of Bangladesh through the distribution of pamphlets at the entrance into EXPO '88 and encouraged people to donate to this worthy cause.

Working collectively with members of the Waiters Union, we held a fundraising dinner dance at the St. Andrews Church Hall in South Brisbane where hundreds attended. We also supported the local Bangladesh community in their own fundraising initiatives. All of this created in us a sense of empathy for those less fortunate. It enabled us to gain a deeper insight into some of the real life struggles facing the people of Bangladesh and assisted in broadening our perspectives to the myriad of challenges facing individuals, families and communities globally.

It was during this time that my eyes and heart were opened to the true spirit and essence of community.

Seeing their work in action throughout the years has given me a good platform to operate from as a Social Work Practitioner. An example of this can be seen in my role as a Community Development Worker at a community centre in Brisbane. I used the skills that I had learnt from the Waiters Union to organise fundraising events which included a dinner dance at the St. Andrews Church Hall to raise funds for the centre. The dinner dance theme was centred around the celebration of our unique cultural identities, where people were encouraged to dress in their traditional clothes.

The catering for the Dinner Dance was a mammoth operation where I also utilised the Waiters approach about sharing and asked twenty of my friends, many of them members of the Waiters Union, to donate to the Dinner Dance by cooking enough food to feed 10 people, which amounts to catering for 200 people. I and my family then cooked enough food to feed 150 people. So all in all we had enough food to feed 350 people.

The Dinner Dance was a great success and we were able to raise approximately $3000 with minimal monetary outlay by the community centre.

Looking back over the years and reflecting on the many roads travelled, through the many faces of change, I have seen the Waiters children grow up, marry and become parents themselves. I have seen the Waiters lose many loved ones, gain new friends and establish new ventures and in all of this the Waiters Union has remained steadfast and strong.

When I think of community, these words spring to mind:

Humility
Honesty
Integrity
Listening to the Silent Voices
Walking the Talk and Talking the Walk
Love
Compassion
Serving the Poor
Caring and Sharing
Supporting the Down Trodden
Engaging the Forgotten Respectfully

These are the core values espoused by the Waiters in their daily pursuit to create community.

I am privileged to have crossed their paths and walked alongside them in my journey of life and it is an honour to call them my friends.

2010

The Waiters Union And Community Development
Peter Westoby

It should be noted that this reflection emerges from approximately seven years of involvement in the Waiters from 1987–1994. During that period I was immersed within neighbourhood work with the Waiters as my base. I then moved to South Africa. Since returning to West End in late 1998 I have only been involved from the perspective of the periphery, engaged in relating to people affiliated to the Waiters network. This reflection then is primarily based on those original seven years of immersion. Things might have changed!

I had been a part of the Waiters for several years when one afternoon I sat down with Dave Andrews and said something like, "We're doing a lot of stuff, getting involved with lots of people – it all feels a bit chaotic and mad." In a nutshell his response was, "there is a method in the madness."

My mention of "madness" and Dave's response about "method" in some way frames how I would like to consider the Waiters Union as a *model* of community development and considering community development as a *method* of social change.

The Waiters is *a* model of community development in the sense of not being *the* model – it reflects the simple reality that there are many ways of understanding community development – and often they need to be constructed from the "bottom-up," acknowledging the diversity of how people might want to

---

Some of Peter's favourite spiritual homes include bookshops, coffee shops, Moreton Island, Mount Barney and Highgate Hill (where he loves living with his partner Larah). His favourite spiritual text is Michael Leunig. At other times he works with either the University of Queensland, where he is a lecturer in community development, or with Community Praxis Co-op. He has spent the past 18 years in community development practice in Australia, South Africa, Vanuatu, PNG and the Philippines.

practise "community" and "development" within the world.

To say that the Waiters is *a*, and not *the* model, does not imply that the Waiters model does not reflect some *orthodoxies* around what normative community development is generally understood to be. The community development of the Waiters is reflective of some key *orthodoxies* that are typical of community development – such as a set of social practices through which people assist, enable, and facilitate groups of people to build relationships, develop analyses and work bottom-up to address issues that are impacting on their lives.

The Waiters is then one model of how people have embodied this set of normative practices. People who are part of the Waiters network purposefully engage in such social practices – assisting others, enabling them, and bringing people together in groups. If nothing else, normative community development is a collective process of social change; it is "stuff" people do *together* to move their private concerns into public processes of deliberation and action.

When I was involved with the Waiters I either observed others, or participated myself in social practices that embodied bringing people together who had mental health problems, women experiencing domestic violence, people wanting to be in solidarity with both refugees and with local Indigenous people. In the coming together of people who shared similar concerns, or similar pain, people were able to support one another in making sense of their world and then choose tactics, strategies or actions that could address some of those pains or concerns.

Ironically, it should also be noted that one important part of the Waiters community development work is that when people come together to develop a "community analysis," sometimes the agreed analysis is to then foster activities and projects that facilitate the opposite of bringing people together in groups. Sometimes the analysis directs the work towards actually helping people who have often been grouped together by the service-delivery industry (e.g. people living in hostels with mental health issues) to see their individual worth through other kinds of friendship within the broader community.

Orthodox community development argues that social change usually does not occur through individual action alone – it requires people creating "community" as groups who together want to bring change. And while the Waiters would agree with that, they would not agree with collapsing the individual into the collective (Buber, 1947) – the individual is considered to be hugely important. The Waiters is an orthodox model of community development that enables collective action that still validates the significance of the individual at the same time.

Having established that the Waiters are doing *orthodox* community development, we need to ask is there anything *unorthodox* – or unique – about the Waiters model?

The Waiters model is *unorthodox* in that it is an *intentional* community development model that is not essentially dependent on any kind of funding or donor. People are a part of the community they work in as people who dream of social change in a very practical sense.

The key *unorthodox* element of the Waiters model is that those who are purposefully engaged in such social change work in the community, are not so much working *for*, or even *with* those who are marginalised, but as people who are actually living *amongst* those people. Some of the other particularities of the

Waiters model can be described as follows.

An *in situ* model whereby people come and participate in the network as citizens who want to learn about doing community development through doing it. There is no sense that people must first becomes "experts" in community development, or accumulate experience elsewhere prior to joining in.

A *relational* model centred on some key ideas/ideals such as *simplicity, solidarity and service*. Such concepts reflect a deep commitment within the model to relational rather than institutional language such as "quality standards," "best practices," and "codes of conduct." Without wanting to disparage the latter, it is important to say that the Waiters, as a non-institutional intentional model of community development are focused on relationally-oriented ideas rather than institutional ideas.

A *reciprocal* model based on *mutual aid*, rather than *service delivery*. People are welcomed-in to receive the support that the Waiters "provide" on the condition they will also reach-out and support others. There is no notion that some are the "professionals" and some are "clients." All are considered to be people with both "resources" and "needs." The Waiters model attempts, as a relational network, to link need to resource as closely as possible.

A *spiritual* model oriented towards a spiritually defined centre, mostly within the Christian tradition, although strongly aligned to a Gandhian interpretation of that tradition. The spiritually defined centre orients the network to put love and justice at the centre of its defining mission.

A *political* model in that there is a genuine effort to construct and maintain an open *anarchist* decision-making process. There are no official leaders, no elected bodies. There are open regular meetings (on Monday mornings at 6.30 am, gatherings, and annual planning days) that people can come to who want to participate in decisions that affect the network.

A *communitarian* model in that it invites people within the network to live up to their own ideals within community. Morality is "constructed" in the context of relationships – one cannot be a moral person as an isolated individual – a case of just-me. Morality is worked out as justice, as opposed to just-me, which can only be measured in the context of community.

The Waiters is not only unique as a model of community development, in my experience its model of community development is also unique as a method of social change.

Firstly, the Waiters practise what I call elsewhere "supportive co-responsibility" (Westoby & Dowling, 2009, p82ff). There is a key recognition that most people change their lives for the better when accompanied by someone else. People who are downtrodden, those who cannot pull themselves up by their bootstraps so to speak – these are the kind of people whom the Waiters try to invite into their lives, or to be invited into. They need help, but not necessarily a patronising help. It is a help forged by relational practice whereby people come alongside one another and hold one another to account in bringing about desired change. Such supportive relational practice has endured for literally decades within the Waiters. People have been supporting one another and holding one another to account in pursuing their desired changes for many many years. And because the whole model is non-dependent on funding and "professional" workers, that is, it is an intentional model, then such long-lasting relational work is possible.

Secondly, in order to practise "supportive co-responsibility" the Waiters practise "networking" – weaving people into a web of relationships that enables people to be both supported and to also provide support – to be accountable and hold others to account, to link people with need to resources as "effectively" as possible.

Thirdly, in order to practise "supportive co-responsibility" in their "networking" the Waiters practise building relationships that are "purposeful." Relationships are forged, groups are nurtured, networks are constructed, with a directional hope – that people will gain more capabilities, and therefore more freedom. There is certainly a lot of sitting around sipping tea, loving coffee, and sharing meals. Such "ordinary" activity is part and parcel of community, but for many within the Waiters there is often purposefulness to this – a conscious commitment to *building* community, with full awareness that within modern society such "ordinary" activity is often undermined by fragmentation, business, mobility and so forth.

Fourthly, the Waiters method is "hospitality-focused" and imbued with a radical hospitality, welcoming the stranger, the "other," the marginal. Within the Waiters model the praxis of such hospitality starts within each person's household, then engages with neighbours, and then with other marginalised people within the neighbourhood.

Fifthly, the Waiters method is "solidarity-oriented" and infused with a spirit of mutuality and standing *alongside* – not of providing a service within the logic of a patron-client relationship. This practice means people within the network are conscious of the damaging impacts of many professionally-defined relationships that are infused with anything but mutuality.

Finally, the Waiters method involves social practices of building "community-oriented structures and processes" that support people's involvement and engagement within the neighbourhood and beyond. Such structures, which are in themselves unique, have been specifically "designed" to support action, rather than take energy away from action. Such processes are minimalist ensuring that people do not waste scarce time participating in an endless spiral of meetings. The Community Initiatives Resource Association, for example, frees people to participate in community and community-oriented activities instead of squashing initiatives and/or sucking time and energy and creativity out of those initiatives.

It is not in having any one of these elements that makes the Waiters unique, it is in the holding of all these elements together that makes the Waiters Union a unique model of community development and *method* of social change.

The Waiters model and method, infused by the practices of love and the hope of justice, are an important contribution to the life of many people in West End, mine included. It is also a model that enables many people in other locations to re-imagine community development in all its breadth and depth and multiplicity.

Buber, M. 1947. *Between Man and Man*. London and New York: Routledge Classics (2002 edition).
Westoby, P. & Dowling. G. 2009. *Dialogical Community Development*. West End: Tafina Press.

2010

The Waiters, Local Power And Community Sustainability
Rob Farago and Russ Holmes

There are many examples of Waiters bringing people together who find they have similar ideals, friendships form, ideas are thrown around, dreams find their voice, experiments begin and something unique spins off that isn't called Waiters but its seed was in the network and is somehow reflective of the network's aspirations of a just, kind and neighbourly society.

That's what happened with Russ Holmes and myself. We connected through various Waiters get togethers after he moved into the area. We started to talk about our emerging interest in environmental sustainability. Russ has a background in building and project management, me in IT and business. My partner was also involved in the dreaming stages and helped out with administration and communications in what became our effort to enhance our community's sustainability – but I am getting ahead of myself.

What turned my attention to sustainability? Climate Change has been the driving factor. Unfortunately at the time of writing, early 2010, the idea of whether people are responsible for Climate Change is polarising the community. In my mind these issues can be reduced to pollution and insurance.

By burning coal we are polluting the atmosphere. Apart from carbon dioxide, burning coal emits other pollutant gasses that cause respiratory problems, as well as toxic heavy metals. Secondly most home owners purchase house insurance in the

---

Rob has lived in West End for 10 years and for 22 years has worked on writing software, building the internet and installing renewable energy, sometimes simultaneously. Russ has a background in the construction industry and currently works full time installing renewable energy in the built environment. He has lived in West End for seven years.

remote likelihood of it burning down. I think it's reasonable for our society to pay a relatively small cost now, akin to insurance, to reduce the risk of large future climate problems, and clean up our energy in the process. While I sincerely hope the climate scientist models are wrong about the future, I am not willing to bet everything by doing nothing.

But I am optimistic. Within my lifetime, I expect Australia to have close to 100% renewable electricity made up of solar (of various types from rooftop and large scale photovoltaic [PV] solar panels, large scale thermal using mirrors to harvest heat to boil water generating electricity even at night time), wind, geothermal etc. With the coming fleet of electric cars, a large proportion of our city driving could also be covered by renewable energy rather than importing fuel from the middle east.

So how did we try to be part of the solution? What we did involved something invisible, powerful and mysterious–God? No. (Though hopefully He's been involved.) I am talking about electricity. We can't see it, but use it every day. It powers much of our lives in cooking, heating water, and washing clothes and so on. However most people don't know much about how it works. We were interested in the idea of putting PV solar panels on our own roofs to make pollution-free electricity, and this led to Local Power being born.

At the time (mid 2007) there were only 342 Queensland homes with PV solar on the grid. Installing solar panels was expensive, even with government rebates. We thought that if we could get the price down through a bulk buy, and thereby entice another 50 or so households to install panels, we would be doing something much more valuable.

We were hoping that greater adoption of PV solar in homes would both boost renewable energy generation and increase our members' "energy consumption literacy" so that they would over time reduce their household's energy use.

We wanted the following specific outcomes for members/participants:

- Significant savings. Not just 10% off the best retail price.
- Good quality installation. This meant using products and installers with a good track record.
- Participation by people who would not otherwise have installed solar panels due to price, complexity or paperwork. The best deal at the time was around $3700. Our aim was to provide a 1kW system under $2000. In the end it was closer to $1500.
- Maximising what participants could purchase. Our 1.5kW systems were not much more than the cost of a 1kW system from other retailers.

We have written in detail in other places (see http://localpower.net.au) about how we managed to get the cost down and the nuts and bolts of what was involved. In summary the cost was lower due to bulk buying components and installation services, and very efficiently working the logistics and administration at lower hourly rates than industry.

However we didn't skimp on quality. We deliberately chose market leading Sharp panels over cheaper Chinese panels. While this option was more expensive, we wanted to have the best chance of the panels lasting the 25 years of their performance warranty and having the supplier company still around.

We hoped that organising as a not for profit community group would encourage participation and reduce fear because we were asking people to pay in full before they had solar panels on their roof. We decided that we would hold a public meeting so that people could get a sense of our honesty and competence.

We must also admit that we were quite staggered that people were willing to give their money to strangers. Apart from several of our friends and neighbours who helped us letterbox drop the entire postcode, we had people who we didn't know delivering flyers in their own suburbs, getting us news coverage, nominating us for an environmental award, and entrusting us with (as of the conclusion of three buying groups) almost five million dollars in funds for 350 homes and 450kW+ of renewable power. We were very encouraged that trust was so high in the first buying group when we had no track record, and we suspect that it came largely from people who were also involved in community and volunteer networks.

As a community based group we were strongly encouraged by experts in academia, industry and government, willing to lend their professional expertise, often in their own time. We were also amazed with the cooperation of our members for the smooth running of the project. We often managed to inspect 12–14 roofs per day in half hour booking slots across Brisbane. Our members were incredibly flexible, sometimes leaving work, or asking friends or relatives to arrange access.

One member wasn't home when we went to inspect, however their neighbour who was also joining in, rang him, found their spare key and let us in. Others helped their elderly neighbours without internet access order online and kept them updated with our email newsletters.

This inspired us to go the extra mile, sometimes literally, to drive to a mail centre late on budget night to post paperwork before a midnight change in government policy. On another occasion we were sent all over a hospital trying to get the signature of a member who was recovering from surgery to once again beat a government policy change.

In forming the first buying group, we found that the respectful relationships of trust we had formed in the locality helped kick start the buying group. Many Waiters households joined in as well as friends, relatives, colleagues and literally our neighbours.

We had to find a home for our buying group. And here again the synergies with Waiters come into play. Community Initiatives Resource Association is not Waiters, but was started by some Waiters to provide a legal, financial and insurance umbrella to Waiters activities and to a vast range of other small informal groups over the years. Local Power was accepted under the umbrella of the Resource Association and it has been a great partnership. We didn't have to incorporate, nor employ a book keeper, and we have the credibility and accountability that comes from being part of a respected not for profit. The Resource Association benefited from the admin fees we collect, which helps out with their bookkeeping and other costs.[11]

We don't pretend that what we are doing is community development. It is not bottom up, consensus based, empowerment focused or inclusive in process. We run it like a small startup where Russ and I make the decisions. Yet we hope our approach reflects something of Waiters. Our work is our vocation and is prompted by our concerns for the most vulnerable on the planet as climate change progresses. Home owners are not the most vulnerable in the community but we have been mindful

---

[11] See "The Community Initiatives Resource Association" in End Notes.

of enabling people of limited means to participate. We want to empower people to make wise changes in their behaviour. We aren't in it to make a fortune, just a reasonable living so that the work is sustainable. We think of our buying group participants as members and not customers. After completing 250 homes, we brought people together to celebrate by sharing some cake, coffee and conversation.

We started this story talking about electricity being invisible, powerful and mysterious. Doing projects in a community context can also be described in the same way. The connections between the people are often invisible. When these connections are harnessed and people work together, sometimes great things can happen. However it seems that there is no set formula that will work every time. There is an element of mystery as to why things fly in one project and don't get off the ground in another.

Local Power – not Waiters Union – but sharing values, plugged into and drawing energy from the Waiters network.

2010

The Waiters, Vibrant Spirituality And Social Justice
Armen Gakavian

An anarchist-turned-Christian-pacifist takes in East Timorese asylum seekers, risking imprisonment. A former Pentecostal pastor teaches carpentry to idle teenagers. A grey-bearded author of books on community resolves a conflict between neighbours. The Catholic Worker household prepares for a visit to the abortion clinic, offering support to mothers facing an unenviable dilemma.

Brisbane's West End was my resting place after a decade-long search for inclusive, non-coercive Christian community. I'd figured that my friends and I were alone in pursuing both vibrant spirituality and social justice. And I'd failed to find more than a handful of faith-based communities that lived out locally the justice they sought globally. My encounter with the Waiters Union in the summer of 1997 was the turning point in my spiritual journey.

I have since discovered dozens of communities like the Waiters Union that pursue spiritual wholeness and engage with issues of local, national and global justice.

We don't know about these communities because they are like the mustard seeds described by Jesus – working quietly, unpretentiously, with no corporate structures or advertising campaigns. These groups find their inspiration in the teachings of Jesus Christ, who called His followers to live lives of unconditional love, whatever the cost; to seek peace, whatever the

---

Armen has extensive experience in facilitating spiritual growth, leadership formation and community development. He has taught leadership, sociology and theological perspectives on social justice in Australia and in the homeland of his ancestors, Armenia. Armen currently lives in Sydney and is involved with The Salvation Army in a housing estate in Sydney's leafy Macquarie Park.

price; and to make the concerns of the marginalised their own, whatever the risks.

Yet the Waiters Union is quite unlike any other community I've come across. The two to three clusters of households in West End are one of the few Christian "frontier" initiatives in Australia, where the difficult issues of faith and life are grappled with, and where answers are found, implemented and constantly re-evaluated in the light of the Spirit of Jesus.

My visit to the Waiters Union was significant, even faith-saving. After years of pondering what authentic faith-in-community might look like in post-modern Australia, I seemed to be left with two choices: Franciscan monasteries and exclusive Christian groups. Was it possible to follow Jesus by serving the community, living simply, sharing possessions and reaching the hidden and forgotten – without the authoritarianism and conformity I had seen in these groups?

The Waiters Union was living proof that this kind of community was possible. It modeled a workable, grace-filled, profoundly Biblical expression of Christ-like engagement with everyday life. My encounter with the community at West End strengthened my resolve to live like Jesus in my local community, both here and overseas (in Armenia) – by putting first those who are considered least, and by constantly evaluating all that I do in the light of Jesus' life and teaching.

Hundreds, if not thousands, of people have been inspired to emulate the principles of the Waiters Union in their own localities. I know of one person who decided to take up part-time work and move into a needy district of Sydney. Several others have created community living arrangements with their friends.

I teach a course on justice and social change. I tell my students that it's not enough to sign petitions and join protests and demonstrations. We can't campaign for social change without "being the change we want to see." But it's also not enough to live justly individually – being kind to others and ethical in our work, installing a water tank in our back yard or buying fair trade coffee. We also need to live out our justice collectively, by creating radically inclusive, non-coercive communities that transform lives and speak prophetically into the mainstream social structures.

Through these communities, we can provide a sample of the better world that we proclaim:

We dream of a world in which all the resources of the earth will be shared equally between all the people of the earth so that even the most disadvantaged among us will be able to meet basic needs with dignity and joy. We dream of a great society of small communities cooperating interdependently to practise personal, social, economic and political compassion, love, justice and peace. ... And we yearn to make this dream a reality in our own locality. (http://www.waitersunion.org/waitersunion.htm)

The key lies in the last sentence. It is possible to create a microcosm of God's new order of justice and "right living" – what the Bible calls the Kingdom of God – smack bang in the middle of mainstream society.

How might this look – not in quiet, multicultural, communitarian West End, but in the bustling inner city, the fast-growing suburban sprawls of our capital cities, the isolated rural communities of outback Australia, and the dilapidated housing estates that have become the "dumping ground" of a system bereft of inspiration? Here are some thoughts.

Wherever I go, I seek out the most marginalized and disadvantaged. These are the people who are excluded from the mainstream, and who lack the skills to make their needs known. We often avoid talking with them because we don't quite know how to relate to them. They may be the socially awkward member of our church, the physically disabled resident in our street, the abused wife who keeps to herself, the neighbour who doesn't speak English, or the lonely old man who sits in the same spot every day in the shopping mall.

These people aren't just found in West End. I live in a middle class suburb in the northwest of Sydney. Here, hidden behind the double brick walls and neatly-kept gardens, there is no lack of brokenness and human tragedy. Mental and physical illness, loneliness, hopelessness and even financial hardship are not the monopoly of the chronically poor.

Then there's the housing estate located just five minutes' drive from my home. Tucked away behind a row of apartment blocks and student housing, Ivanhoe Place Estate is located across the road from leafy Macquarie University and the Baptist Theological College, and around the corner from Australia's fastest growing CBD. The Estate is home to 1,000 residents ranging from low income and single-parent families through to the mentally ill and recovering addicts. In my search for my city's most marginalized, I have joined The Salvation Army team that has been bringing hope and healing to these residents for over a decade. Despite, or perhaps because of, their brokenness and vulnerability, my friends in the Estate express their Christian faith and commitment to their community in ways I have rarely seen before.

Jesus attracted a motley crew of the socially despised, the sick, the confused, the cynical and the "sinner." He welcomed them, embraced them and transformed them into the leaders of a movement that would change the world. Jesus didn't just call for governments to act more justly; He modeled God's justice by forming an egalitarian community, where the last were first, and the first were last; where serving one another was considered a joy and a privilege, not a chore; and where material, social and human resources were placed at the disposal of those who needed them the most. The religious and political powers-that-be did not know what to do with this movement; their response ranged from indifference to sarcasm to violent persecution.

I try to live locally the justice that I seek globally. I have preached about the need to welcome the stranger. I have signed petitions calling for better access for the physically disabled. I have placed a virtual ribbon on my Facebook profile in solidarity with abused women. I have written a letter to the newspaper opposing racism. And I am co-founder of an Australian charity that raises funds for the refugees, disabled and elderly in faraway Armenia.

Good and helpful as all of this is, it's relatively easy to advocate for someone we've never met. It's another thing to personally care for, listen to and speak up for the marginalized and disadvantaged in our own communities. The effectiveness of our advocacy is multiplied tenfold when we offer a credible sample of the alternative we proclaim. As we embrace the forgotten ones, we model a new social order, the Kingdom of God, based on justice and right living. Both personal and collective engagement are crucial if we are to deliver *locally* the justice that we work towards *globally*.

I see every corporate spiritual activity as a proclamation of justice. We often think of "spiritual" activity as something detached from everyday life. For example, we think of church services solely as an opportunity to withdraw from the outside world and engage in reflective experiences that satisfy our spiritual longing and ease our physical and emotional pain. But this is only part of the picture.

Any spiritual activity carried out in Jesus' name is by nature an act of *dissent against* the social order, and an *affirmation of* the values of the Kingdom of God and of all that is good and just. We proclaim this Kingdom every time we meet in egalitarian fellowship with people of different classes, gender, and ethnic and religious backgrounds; every time we welcome the stranger in our midst and offer forgiveness, healing and hope; every time we speak and sing the Scriptures; every time we share the bread and wine. And so any gathering that *reflects on* the life and teachings of Jesus must also *reflect* the life and teachings of Jesus.

Each of the activities of the Waiters Union – the Monday morning time of worship, reflection and planning, the mid-week home groups, Sunday nights in the basement of St Andrew's Anglican church, the fortnightly community meal – proclaims the values of God's Kingdom, not just through the words spoken, but also through the diversity and active involvement of participants. I'm constantly challenged to view our own corporate spiritual activities at Ivanhoe Place in the light of this model and to ensure that those activities reflect the values of the Kingdom of God, both in *content* and *form*.

The Waiters Union challenges us to shape our faith communities around the needs of the most marginalized and disadvantaged. To express locally the justice that we seek globally, by embracing and advocating for those least esteemed by society. And to ensure that our corporate spiritual activities are consistent with our values and provide tangible evidence of the justice-based alternative that we preach. These are the building blocks of the better world of which we dream.

2010

The Experience Of Pain And The Possibility Of Change
Maddie Anlezark

In 1986 I was at university studying for a degree in social work. My journey to this point in my life had been a tough one. I was abused physically, emotionally and sexually. As a young adult I ran from my family to Australia. I then married an alcoholic who was abusive and sometimes violent, and had just left him.

I had tried incredibly hard to please God, just as I tried hard to please my parents, but increasingly I believed that I failed and could not succeed. Sometimes I felt that the picture that I had of God as stern judge was not the true or whole picture. I also feared that I was wrong and that God was indeed deeply disappointed with me and saw me as a failure. Gradually it became too painful to think about God and I stopped going to church, prayed seldom, and yearned for somebody who would love me. Now I had broken marriage vows to add to my failures.

Dave Andrews was one of my social work tutors. He introduced himself as a follower of Jesus, who had recently been living in India with his wife and children, living with drug addicts and people with psychiatric conditions. He encouraged us to look at our values and our dreams of how we would like the world to be, and consider how we could help to make this happen. As he talked I became excited and glimpsed a God who really cared about people and was on the side of those who hurt and struggled. This was also disturbing because it made me think about my life and about God and enter again into the confusion against which I had insulated myself. However, it resonated with

---

Maddie currently lives in England near her sister and quite close to where she was born West of London. She works as a social worker with older people in hospital discharge but will soon be retiring so that she has time and energy for all her commitments in her local community.

something deep inside me and I could not ignore it.

One Saturday I felt desperate and could not work out how I could carry on, begin again to try and work out what life is all about, or even manage to survive. I went to the telephone box and dialled Dave's number and when he answered I cried and told him I needed to speak to someone. He drove over and got me, took me to his home, introduced me to his wife and children, made a cup of tea, and they sat with me around their kitchen table. I began to weep bitterly, reached out and clutched them and asked them to hold on to me.

After I had cried for some time Dave asked me if I would mind if he prayed for me. He told God that my heart was broken into tiny pieces and that I did not see that it could ever be put back together. He asked God to show me that God could mend my broken heart and would do so, not necessarily by changing the circumstances of my life, but from within my heart. It was as if I was physically jolted and had found the God I had been looking for all my life, though I did not really understand what it meant. I could not believe that these people had tried to understand my pain and that they thought there was life ahead for me despite the death of so many of my hopes.

I began to get involved with some of the things they were doing with marginalised people in our neighbourhood, particularly refugees and people living in psychiatric hostels. My progress was slow and stumbling, the pain was sometimes excruciating, but I was starting to find a God who loved me, called me to follow him and could cope with the mess that my life had been so far. I struggled frequently with doubts and I was scared of trusting God and of trusting the new people in my life because all my past experience screamed at me that I would only get hurt again. It was like a fight went on inside me. I can remember saying on several occasions that knowing God certainly did not make life painless, but it did make it possible to go on and believe for a better future.

After a while, I moved into the Bristol Street household where people learned to live out their Christian values with those on the margins of our local community. Here I learned a great deal more about God and learned gradually to trust the people with whom I lived. It was still a real struggle for me to trust and living with others at very close and crowded quarters brought home to me how broken I was. It must have been very difficult for them to live with me when I was so easily hurt, did not really trust them or believe that they wanted me to be with them, and spent a great deal of the time crying bitterly as I got in touch with my pain and brokenness.

However these amazing people, younger than me, loved me and nurtured me and truly accepted me. I learned with these people how to begin to live out the dream of creating with God the kind of world that we wanted to live in, and I got in touch with dreams I had had long ago but been unable to carry through. Still I had times when I pushed people away when they got too close, even those who showed me the greatest love, because I was scared and thought that it would be easier to push them away before they discovered that I was not the kind of person they wanted to associate with and rejected me.

My journey with God continued and a highlight was when I was asked by the residents of Bristol Street house to be their external supervisor (I was no longer living at Bristol Street by then). This entailed attending a weekly household meeting, and spending regular time with the female residents each week.

My role was to help them both communally and individually to be clear about their dreams, to sort out differences between household members, and to seek ways of demonstrating God's love for each other and those in our local community.

Two of the people living in the house during the time of my involvement were Dave and Ange Andrews who had played such a pivotal role in my discovery of the truth of who God is. I think that it was a watershed in my understanding of the Christian life, and an encouragement to us all, to realise that this "wounded healer," me, could be used by God to pastor others, even those who had been her pastors in the past. God's ideas of role definition are so much more open and fluid than those so often adopted by society, and unfortunately by many churches.

Later, I worked as a colleague with Dave on a project with women who had been sexually abused as children within church run orphanages. This too we experienced as an amazing testimony of God's healing power and the true possibilities for freedom within the Christian life.

I have now been back in England for seven and a half years and all that I learned with the Waiters has led me on in my journey with Christ. I am part of a team that runs a course called "Workshop" encouraging people to look at what it means to follow Christ and make our world the kind of place God intends it to be.

With Street Pastors I go out on the streets of Kingston on Friday or Saturday night and walk around talking to those out, chatting, building relationship, helping out if needed. With some friends I help to organise a group at our local homeless hostel to befriend and support each other, share our dreams and struggles, talk about Christ, develop relationship with God and pray together.

The Experience Of Pain And The Possibility Of Change

Once a year we go with our friends from the hostel to Greenbelt, a Christian festival, and camp together for a long weekend. We have just started a Sunday afternoon group where we share food, friendship, activities, talk about God and pray together with anyone in our neighbourhood who wants to come.

When I met Dave I was broken and defeated and most of my dreams had died. Now I live in hope of the world that God will complete as his kingdom. All the adventures I am undertaking in England, all the dreams I have, my motivation and my values were affirmed, developed, experimented with and nurtured by my friends in the Waiters in Brisbane, Australia.

My vision and strength come from God but I could not persevere in it without the knowledge that all these friends are sharing with me. Through my experience with Waiters Union God transformed me and showed me how to work with him to transform his world and to enable others to know his transforming, redemptive love and compassion.

2010

Being The Change We Want To See In The World
Cara Munroe

I don't remember exactly how it came about. It's not about one big act of conversion. It's more about osmosis. The collective wisdom of the Waiters Union crossing the barriers of heart and mind through daily acts of kindness and listening.

Somewhere, perhaps in the chaotic Sunday night services at St Andrews or perhaps Heretics Corner bible study or perhaps even under the house with Nick, rolling cigarettes I learnt this: you don't need to change the whole world. Within your own sphere of influence is a whole world awaiting change. Start with you.

And at the Bristol Street household that's what we were encouraged to do. My angry revolutionary leanings were slowly sullied by shared pots of tepid coffee and the tedious microcosmic task of learning to build relationships. Dismantle internal prejudices. Be loving.

I was angry in those days. Angry and ranty. Still, in my annoying rantyness I was accepted, and acceptance is contagious.

I left the Waiters Union in 2005. Still a little unsure of what it had all meant, but fortified with hope and a new plan of action. It was Gandhi who said it first, but it feels paved into the streets of West End: Be the change you wish to see in the world.

Fast forward. Two years later.

A prison, Victoria's only maximum security women's prison. A place where everyone wears a uniform. Compelled to work along-

---

Cara has lived in intentional community in Malaysia, India, West End and most recently Footscray, Melbourne where she is part of the Footscray Church of Christ. She is a registered nurse and, inspired by the Waiters Union, passionate believer in shared meals and cups of tea.

side women detained inside, I have accepted a job as a nurse in the medical centre.

Four times a day muster, the term used to describe a headcount of cattle, is called, and the headcount of women is commenced. Each prisoner is required to cease what they are doing and stand at the heavy metal door of their cell with their ID waiting for their name to be ticked off.

Medication is dispensed three times a day. Women wait with their ID in a long winding queue outside the barred pharmacy window and small plastic cups of anti-psychotics, Metamucil and Panadol are slid under.

Nurse clinic is run every morning from 10.00 am. Prisoners sit in the magazine-less waiting room for their seven minutes alone with a nurse. Almost routinely, after a few gentle questions, a dull ache in the stomach turns into a disclosure of years of sexual assault, an upcoming family court hearing, worry that an infant daughter is now, in turn, being abused.

Staff members overtly expressing empathy or seen going out of their way to help a prisoner out are mockingly labelled "care bears."

Meals are issued from the main kitchen, at 11.00 am and 4.00 pm, in plastic takeaway tubs or damp paper bags. Sometimes there are court escorts, or visits, or someone overdoses on heroin or weaves a metal paperclip through their eyelid and needs to be sent, handcuffed, to hospital.

Usually there is nothing. And the nothingness is what weighs most heavily. On the prisoners, on the staff. On me.

After almost six months, aside from regularly flouting the uniform policy and making a point of calling everybody by name (not number) I feel I haven't achieved anything.

Still, my ranty left wing idea of prison officers as belching uniformed Simpsons characters has been transformed, and I now know them as people with whom I exchange recipes and share my lunch.

With the prisoners, the days of sizing up and being sized up lessening, I now happily share prison banter or a cup of super strong coffee, accept compliments about my green shoes or colourful skirt and occasionally teach a newbie to circumvent some red tape or roll a cigarette.

But within my little sphere of influence, things had been changing.

The prison medical centre, undergoing an image overhaul, needed to put something on its annual report to do with spiritual health. Identified as the nurse most suited to that sort of unscientific task, the portfolio was offered to me. And so the weekly sacred space, or "meditation with nurse Cara" as it became known amongst the prison community, was born.

The idea was simple. A weekly space set apart as a place of rejuvenation within the confines of the prison walls. Each week was a different theme and ended in a herbal "tea ceremony" requiring preparation, props and help to organise.

Outside the prison, an inspired Sally handed over prized pieces of her wedding crockery to use as part of the sessions, Kemmy seeing dried chrysanthemum flowers and rose buds at the Asian grocers added them to her shopping trolley hoping they may be of use. Ben and Marcus burnt CDs of meditational music and typed pages explaining their selections and my mum donated expensive packets of gourmet herbal tea. Aurin, my Muslim next door neighbour, followed keenly the progress of the group, leaving post-it notes of encouragement on my front door.

It was inside the prison, however, that the officers, whose kids' names I had spent six months learning and whom I gave shoulder massages to on stressful days opened doors that, from the outset appeared sealed over and bricked shut.

At the gatehouse, the Prison Officers (POs) who were responsible for all that entered and left the prison, and presided over a clunking x-ray machine and large metal detector, greeted armfuls of autumn leaves, tubes of paint, throw cushions and assorted CDs with occasional "Om" sounds and approximation of the lotus position. Then followed by swift security clearance and best wishes for the day ahead.

POs S and J always gave me a razz about herbal teas, but never failed to help me carry the chinking tea set.

PO C who accusingly called the women "crims" and me a "care bear" radioed through to the control tower for PA announcements about the meditation group and lent me a CD player from the Officers station.

PO T, a naturopath in a past life, photocopied pages from her own collection of aromatherapy books and surreptitiously sprayed lavender water around the common areas before and after meditation group to promote calm.

Administrator K rostered me onto shifts when the prison was at its most quiet and sessions would face the least interruptions and Nurse C covered my clinics while I ran the sessions and instructed other nurses to do likewise.

And when the intrusive "muster" is announced, POs S and P overlook the policy which requires all women to return to their cell door and check off the muster list silently from outside the meditation room.

All were implicated in the conspiracy of hope.

Over the next 18 months a small group of women prisoners and I launched origami boats of hope, prayed the Hebrew "breath of God," hand stitched Tibetan prayer flags, built symbolic birds' nests, water coloured dreamy mandalas, and traced Celtic labyrinths.

We would end each session with a shared pot of herbal tea and a chance to talk and reflect. Peach, peppermint and Turkish apple. The smells of far off times and places. Pouring became an act of hospitality and of blessing. We never poured for ourselves and our cups were never drunk to emptiness.

The women began to queue at the medication window, not for a Panadol, but to ask when the next meditation group was to be held.

And now POs J and K and some of the nurses are asking me to run a meditation session for them.

"I don't have the time to run a separate one at this stage, but if you asked the women beforehand, I'm sure they wouldn't mind you joining in."

On his lunch break PO J taps on the door and enters, hat in hand. Addressing the whole group, he asks if he may sit with us.

A pause.

L beams warmly in his direction and with a "Sit here Mr J" indicates towards a spare yoga mat. The usually antagonistic B offers him her own cushion, another woman pours him a herbal tea from the communal pot.

Together we sit.

Prison Officer, Prisoners and Nurse.

At the end of the session, with the quiet strains of Puccini punctuating his movements PO J moves his large mass up of the floor and humbly returning his cup, thanks us all.

In that moment, what I can only describe as the same spirit that can be felt amongst the Waiters Union transcended those prison walls.

Epilogue.

Lack of nursing staff. Lack of resources. Lack of energy.

The meditation program has now ground out to nothing.

PO T has been redeployed to the gatehouse and aside from a fading vase of lavender stalks, life in the compound grinds on, for all I can tell, pretty much as before.

Two days ago, picking up my partner from his work place at a city library, I sit leafing through a book when one of the last customers to leave approaches me. "Nurse Cara?"

Out of uniform, I didn't recognise J who had spent 22 months on remand at the prison. She engulfs me in a big perfumed hug.

As the door is locked and last of the books shelved, we exchange stories about life on the inside and the outside.

She gives me another big hug. And another.

As the members of the meditation group trickle back into the community, I hope to one day see each of them again. Meet on mutual terms, perhaps share a cup that need never be empty. J and I wish one another the very best.

I wonder if, perhaps, a little of the world has changed after all.

2010

End Notes

Waiters Union Liturgy

Many people would say the Waiters Union is more of a dream than a reality – an aspiration rather than an accomplishment- something we are working towards rather than something we have already created. This is reflected in The Liturgy For Community posted on our website.[12]

> The Waiters Union is a network of residents
> working towards community in our locality,
> so as to realise the love of God for all people,
> particularly those on the periphery of our society.
>
> Our example is Jesus of Nazareth,
> whose way of life serves as the inspiration
> for the simple, practical and compassionate path
> we want to take in relation to the planet.
>
> Our hope would be that we would not slavishly copy Jesus,
> but would voluntarily make the same choices Jesus made,
> to accept life, respect life, and empower people to live
> life to the full.
>
> We want to know God, the source of life, more fully.
> We would like to cultivate the disciplines
> that would help us develop a relationship to God
> in the midst of our ordinary everyday lives.
> We would seek to live in harmony with the heart of God,
> sustaining ourselves, supporting one another, and serving
> those around about us
> in an increasingly steadfast, faithful, life affirming manner.

---

[12] http://www.waitersunion.org/liturgy.htm.

We want to be aware of ourselves,
and the gift of life, that each of us can bring to this community.
We recognise not only the reality of our weaknesses,
but also the reality of our strengths.
And we would seek to grow individually as people,
in our capacity for self-care, self-control, and self-sacrifice,
for the sake of the community.

We want to be aware of one another,
and the gift of life, that every one else can bring
to this community.
We acknowledge not only the reality of our brokenness,
but also our potential for wholeness in relationships.
And we would seek to grow collectively as people,
in our capacity to speak truthfully, listen attentively,
and work cooperatively,
for the sake of the community.

We particularly want to remember people in the community
who are neglected, rejected or forgotten.
We would like to affirm our commitment
to the welfare of the whole of the human family.
And we would seek to make ourselves available,
to brothers and sisters who are marginalized,
in their ongoing struggle for love and justice.

We disagree about many things,
but one thing we agree on:
the need for us to join together,
to develop a community in our locality,
that is more devoted, more inclusive, and more nonviolent.

2001

Waiters Union Activities

The Waiters Union mobilises many volunteers to participate in many local community groups – which may or may not identify with the Waiters Union. Examples of past activities people from the network were involved in include setting up the Queensland edition of The Big Issue, a national newspaper sold by homeless people as an employment-generation project; coordinating the inner-city inter-church Room in The Inn crash beds pilot program for homeless women at risk in Brisbane; and developing the Hail and Ride Bus Service which is now run by the Brisbane City Council which provides affordable transport to the shops, hospitals and social services in the area.

At the time of writing, activities supporting and/or supported by people in the Waiters Union include:

1. An annual planning day – a day of planning attended by around 30 to 40 people.

2. Network gatherings – three hour networking gatherings of up to 15 people held every six weeks.

3. Coordinating meetings – one hour coordinating meetings of up to five people every week.

4. Ongoing involvement with Aboriginal people in association with Aunty Jean, a local Aboriginal leader.

5. Ongoing involvement with refugees in association with the West End Migrant and Refugee Support Group, Refugee Airfare Loans Scheme (RALS), the Refugee Sewing Group, and Ethical Property Management (EPM) – a social enterprise which aims to generate employment

with refugees.

6. Ongoing involvement in interfaith dialogue through Misbah (a Christian interfaith dialogue initiative that we started) in association with AMARAH (Australian Muslims Advocating the Rights of All Humanity).

7. Ongoing involvement with people in public housing, boarding houses, and hostels.

8. Ongoing involvement with global justice issues through Servants, TEAR, Make Poverty History, Make Indigenous Poverty History and the Micah Challenge.

9. Ongoing involvement in and support for alternative local economic ventures such as Justice Products, Blackstar Coffee Roastery, and Ethical Property Management.

10. Ongoing involvement in and support for alternative local environmental ventures such as Local Power, which installs PV solar panels to generate electricity sustainably.

11. Community meals – a fortnightly evening meal in a local church hall, usually attended by about 40 to 50 people who bring food to share. The majority live in local supported accommodation hostels; some, who were relocated from their accommodation in West End as one of the consequences of the gentrification, come from Carindale to attend.

12. Community picnics – regular picnics or similar outings are arranged for 10 to 25 people who live in hostels or different forms of supported accommodation.

13. Community transport – using a minibus people are rostered on each week to provide transport for about 20 people who would otherwise have difficulty attending activities.

14. Community fellowship – an evening service held at St Andrews Anglican Church, South Brisbane, for about 40 to 50 people, that provides people, particularly those who do not usually have the opportunity, with the opportunity to contribute to a church service, through leading, presenting, praying, sharing and so on.

15. Community Orientation Course – an intensive live-in course focusing on practical community involvement within a Christian community development framework with many of the more marginalised local groups and individuals. Courses are for two weeks mid year and at the end of the year, involving about a dozen participants each time.

16. Community households – like the Princhester Street household and its predecessor, the Bristol Street household, which provide people with opportunities to learn about intentional community and community involvement with marginalised local residents, giving support in the form of friendship, assistance with living skills, conflict resolution, advocacy, and so on. Other group households spring up organically from time to time linked to the network, with an intentional community focus.

17. Project Hope – a support network for church based

community workers in south east Queensland, involving a meeting each six weeks attended by 20 to 30 people.

18. Soup and Doco Evenings – once a fortnight people go dumpster diving, make veggie soup and show hot-topic contemporary documentaries attended by up 20 people.

19. Study, Reading and Theology Groups – three or four groups with up to 20 people in each discuss a range of materials on theology, community, politics and economics. Some are short term, others ongoing.

20. Support groups, both regular and adhoc, such as the men's group and a women's group.

21. End of year camp – a weekend camp attended by around 50 adults and children.

2010

The Community Initiatives Resource Association

The Waiters Union has always been a non-formal community network, but over time we came to recognise the need for a formal community organisation as an auspice for some of our community activities.

Usually groups solve this problem by turning their non-formal community network into a formal community organisation, but in the move towards institutionalisation, they lose the very charisma of community. The free and flexible, strong but gentle spirit of the community that they started out with, ends up being bound hand and foot by rules and regulations and becoming a slave to the system that it sought to overthrow.

So we decided that we would not institutionalise our community under any circumstances. Instead we set up a formal organisation as a parallel structure alongside the non-formal network, so that if anyone in the community needed an officially-recognised, legally-registered auspice for certain activities, they could use the Community Initiatives Resource Association ("The Resource Association").

In line with this vision, the Resource Association Management Committee works in a spirit of servanthood, empowering Waiters Union and other groups who seek its support, rather than having its own agenda and co-opting groups and their activities to drive that agenda. In this spirit, it has helped establish many community programs; through providing healthy guidance, services, and accountability; without unhealthy control.

Since its inception the Resource Association has managed the finances for community property, provided compulsory public liability insurance, become the employer for people whose grants have required that arrangement, and supplied workers and volunteers with the cover that they require to carry community based projects.

The Resource Association has also helped establish many community groups, some on their way to becoming their own incorporated association (including some which are now very prominent in the local community and/or community sector), some who have remained informal groups, others which had a finite life. These groups include Micah Projects, the Creative Stress Solutions Project, the Inner City Citizens Advocacy Group, the Praxis Community Cooperative, West End Community Association (WECA) and Spiral Community Hub.

The Training Team is currently a program that is run by the Resource Association using funds provided by the Uniting Church of Australia through a Vision For Mission.

2010

The Community Praxis Co-op

The Community Praxis Co-op is a not-for-profit workers cooperative that was established in 1998 by a group of community development colleagues who were part of the Waiters Union. There are currently nine members of the Co-op, and a network of more than fifty colleagues from a range of community backgrounds, who work together on a range of projects.

Community Praxis Co-op exists to empower people and to resource and strengthen the capacities of groups and organisations in developing peaceful, just and sustainable communities and operates as an education, training and consultancy agency for individuals, neighbourhoods, non-government organisations, and government authorities.

The Community Praxis Co-op was originally auspiced through the Resource Association and while it still includes people who are also part of the Waiters Union, it is a completely autonomous agency with no formal association with the Waiters Union as such.

Much of the training philosophy and many of the training materials and resources and programs which the Community Praxis Co-op uses were developed in the Waiters Union.

However whereas the training delivered in the Waiters Union is specifically aligned to the Christian tradition and explicitly articulated as Christ-centred, the training delivered by the Co-op is not. The training delivered by the Co-op is more generic community work training.

The Co-op seeks to practise traditional cooperative principles, encouraging the development of acceptance and respect, spirituality and compassion, solidarity and participation, responsibility and competence in individuals, neighbourhoods and organisations.

2010

www.ingramcontent.com/pod-product-compliance
Lightning Source LLC
Chambersburg PA
CBHW070249230426
43664CB00014B/2457